COURAGEOUS CHRISTIANS

COURAGEOUS CHRISTIANS

DEVOTIONAL STORIES FOR FAMILY READING

Joyce Brown

MOODY PRESS

CHICAGO

Scripture taken from the *Holy Bible: New International Version*®. NIV®. Copyright © 1973, 1978, 1984 by International Bible Society. Used by permission of Zondervan Publishing House. All rights reserved.

ISBN: 0-8024-4348-6

1 3 5 7 9 10 8 6 4 2

Printed in the United States of America

With love to my personal hero—my husband, David—and to our sons,
Ryan and Phillip. Thank you for all your support and help.
I also want to express heartfelt gratitude to friends and family
who prayed this book into being.

CONTENTS

AUTHOR'S NOTE

Like many moms, I dream big dreams for my children. Not that I care if they achieve prominence or make much money. Rather, I dream that they will know God intimately and love Him with every inch of their being. That they will learn to listen for His voice and be ready to follow His directions, no matter what the cost. That they will glorify God and bring light to a world that sorely needs it.

While I pray to be a good example, my life isn't as inspiring as I wish it were. I've often wished my sons could be surrounded by genuine heroes. But in today's world, heroes seem to be in shorter supply than they once were. James Dobson has said we are desperately in need of inspiring Christian models with which our young people can identify. Chuck Colson has said that we live in an age of celebrities rather than heroes; our society often idolizes people who are famous even if their character is sadly lacking.

The idea to combine family devotional readings and inspiring biographies grew out of a need in our own family. As our children reached the upper elementary grades and beyond, we struggled to find devotional materials that appealed to them. They complained about illustrations they felt had been fabricated to make a point. I realized that true stories about real Christians would have a greater impact.

My subjects are from different parts of the world, from the past, and from the present. They are men, women, and children with resilient spirits, mountain-moving faith, goosebump courage, and selfless, sacrificial love. People with hearts on fire for the Lord.

I believe their stories will change lives, because writing them has changed mine. A. W. Tozer wrote: "Next to the Holy Scriptures the greatest aid to the life of faith may be Christian biography. It is indeed notable that a large part of the Bible itself is given over to the life and labors of prophets, patriarchs, and kings—who they were, what they did and said, how they prayed and toiled and suffered and triumphed at last!"[1]

While doing the research for this book, I noted how often one believer was influenced by the life of another. Josh McDowell dedicated his life to serving God after reading about Jim Elliot's life. Dorie Van Stone decided to become a missionary after hearing Darlene Diebler speak about her experiences. William Carey and David Livingstone were deeply touched by David Brainerd's biography. Kenneth Taylor's life was changed by reading Bill Borden's story. George Muller was inspired to start his work with orphans after reading a book about August Franke. Amy Carmichael was often encouraged by George Muller's story. As a college sophomore, Cameron Townsend was impressed by Hudson Taylor's biography and embarked on his own mission career soon after. The list goes on. It's my prayer that the following stories will cause that list to continue to grow.

Because the Christians in *Courageous Christians* are from different time periods and parts of the world, historical and geographical lessons will be learned as well. So that the book may be used by families with children of different ages, I have occasionally provided brief definitions following words that younger children might not understand.

1

CORRIE ten BOOM

THEN PETER CAME TO JESUS AND ASKED, "LORD,
HOW MANY TIMES SHALL I FORGIVE MY BROTHER
WHEN HE SINS AGAINST ME? UP TO SEVEN TIMES?"
JESUS ANSWERED, "I TELL YOU, NOT SEVEN TIMES, BUT
SEVENTY-SEVEN TIMES." (MATTHEW 18:21–22)

Corrie ten Boom was born in Holland in 1892, the youngest child in a loving Christian family whose hearts, hands, and home were always open to anyone in need. As she grew older, it was only natural that Corrie also reached out to those around her. In addition to working in her father's watch repair shop, she started Christian clubs for girls, worked with the mentally retarded, helped care for foster children, and taught Bible lessons in the schools.

After Germany invaded Holland in World War Two, helping the people who needed her aid became very dangerous. Germany's cruel dictator, Adolph Hitler, sent soldiers to Holland to round up all the Jewish people and take them to prison camps, where they were later killed by the millions. Anyone found helping the Jews could suffer the same fate.

But Corrie and her family could not turn their backs on people in need. They became part of the Dutch "underground" movement, which hid Jews and helped them escape to safer places.

The ten Booms built a secret room in their home with a hidden panel to open it. They put in an alarm system so that they could quickly buzz a warning throughout the house. They also had the Jews who stayed with them practice disappearing quickly into the secret room.

Corrie and her team of eighty workers helped hundreds of Jews escape before a fellow Dutchman turned them in to the Germans. On February 28, 1944, German soldiers stormed into the ten Boom home. One of them asked Corrie where they were hiding the Jews. When she didn't answer, he slapped her again and again. She and her family were arrested and taken to different prison camps. Her father, who was quite old, died ten days later.

After three months, Corrie was moved to Ravensbruck, a well-known death camp for women. There she was reunited with her sister, Betsie. Ravensbruck was their worst nightmare come true: long hours of very hard work; crowded, rat-filled, unheated buildings; little food; and cruel guards. Before the war ended, 96,000 women died there.

A guard once hit Corrie in the neck with a whip when she was too sick to push a heavy cart. But the hardest thing for her was seeing Betsie mistreated. Betsie had never been healthy. In prison she became much worse. Still, she was forced to keep working and to stand at attention for hours at a time in bitterly cold weather.

Their strong faith in God helped them get through each terrible day. They lovingly reached out to the other women, encouraged them to trust God, and prayed together. Even in that awful place, they felt God's love. In fact, Betsie told Corrie that they would travel all over after they got out, telling people that no place on earth is so dark that God's love cannot shine into it. She also hoped to start homes in Holland and Germany where people broken by the war could heal.

Betsie never saw her dreams come true. She died in prison. But Corrie went on to carry out her sister's wishes. Corrie was set free because of a typing error—which she said was a miracle—shortly before the other women her age were killed.

After the war, she went to Germany. She spoke to large groups there, telling them about the hope God had given her and how Jesus can help us forgive our enemies and even love them.

One day after speaking, she stood at the door shaking hands with people. A man walked up to her and told her he had become a Christian after the war. Corrie recognized the man. He had been one of the cruelest guards at Ravensbruck. The man said he knew God had forgiven him for everything he had done in the past, but he wanted her forgiveness, too.

As he held out his hand, Corrie remembered the misery he had caused Betsie and thousands of others. She wrestled with her answer. She didn't think she could forgive him, but she knew God wanted her to. Silently she prayed, *Lord, I can take his hand, but I can't change my feelings. Only You can do that.*

She took his hand in hers, and a sudden feeling of warmth went through her arm and then her whole body, melting the bitter memories. With tears in her eyes, she told the man who had once tormented her, "I forgive you with all my heart."[1]

DISCUSS

What is the worst thing anyone ever did to you? Have you forgiven that person? What is the worst thing you've ever done to someone else? Have you asked that person to forgive you?

2

TREVOR FERRELL

"A MAN WAS GOING DOWN FROM JERUSALEM TO
JERICHO, WHEN HE FELL INTO THE HANDS OF ROB-
BERS. THEY STRIPPED HIM OF HIS CLOTHES, BEAT HIM
AND WENT AWAY, LEAVING HIM HALF DEAD.... BUT A
SAMARITAN, AS HE TRAVELED, CAME WHERE THE MAN
WAS; AND WHEN HE SAW HIM, HE TOOK PITY ON HIM.
HE WENT TO HIM AND BANDAGED HIS WOUNDS,
POURING ON OIL AND WINE. THEN HE ... TOOK HIM
TO AN INN AND TOOK CARE OF HIM." (LUKE 10:30, 33–34)

Trevor Ferrell was watching the evening news a few weeks before Christmas of 1983 when he first heard about the homeless people who lived on the streets. Trevor was eleven years old at the time. He couldn't believe there were really people who slept outside in the winter in his own city of Philadelphia.

After his parents told him the story was true, he bombarded them with questions: "You mean they have no place to sleep, no home? They're out there in the cold and snow right now? Where do they eat? How do they stay alive without a bed and a blanket?"[1]

When his parents couldn't answer his questions, Trevor asked one more: "Well, can we go downtown and help them?"

Tired and not sure it was safe for their young son to visit the homeless at night, they said no. But Trevor kept asking. As Christians, Mr. and Mrs. Ferrell had always tried to teach their children to care about others. This was a chance to help their son do just that. Finally they agreed and made a short trip that would change all of their lives.

Trevor saw a shoeless man sleeping on a metal grate. He got out of the car and politely offered the man a yellow blanket and the special pillow he had always slept with. The memory of the man's happy smile made him ask his parents to take him back a couple of nights later. This time he took along one of his mother's old coats and gave it to a woman who was shivering from the cold.

Soon the Ferrells were driving downtown night after night. On each trip, Trevor took gifts for the homeless—blankets, sweaters, coats, and food. As he gave his gifts, he always took time to talk and be friendly. Since the street people were usually ignored because of the way they looked, his friendship meant as much to them as his gifts. He became a symbol of hope and caring to the homeless. They called him "Little Buddy" and looked for him nightly.

Then people heard about what the Ferrells were doing and started bringing them coats, blankets, and food to pass on to the men and women on the street. After their story was told in the papers, on the news, and on many talk shows, their nightly visits grew into "Trevor's Campaign." As many as seventy families took turns feeding more than one hundred homeless people each night from a donated van. Later, an old hotel was donated, too. After repairs and remodeling, it became Trevor's Place, a home for the homeless. All because one boy cared enough to get involved.

It wasn't all smooth sailing for the Ferrells along the way. The publicity and the rapid growth of a ministry they hadn't planned on turned their lives upside down for a time. Other children at school made fun of Trevor by calling him "Mr. Superstar" and asking if he had a blanket for them.

Trevor also had a learning disability that made reading difficult. Normally he worked on schoolwork at night to keep up with his class. As he spent more and more time helping the homeless, Trevor got behind in school and had to repeat the sixth grade.

Trying to run Trevor's Campaign, organize volunteers, and collect and distribute donations while caring for their own family and business wore Mr. and Mrs. Ferrell out. But the more they got to know the homeless people, the more they understood their problems and the more they wanted to help them. So one day Trevor's father decided to trust God, close the television repair business he had owned for nineteen years, and run Trevor's Campaign full time.

Through all the difficulties, the joy of helping the needy kept them going—bringing help, hope, and friendship to the homeless of Philadelphia.

DISCUSS

There are people in desperate need in faraway places, and we can help them only through our prayers or financial gifts. But there are also needy people nearby whom we can help personally, if we are willing to go out of our way as Trevor and the Good Samaritan did. Think of some people in your town, church, or neighborhood going through hard times. How could you help them?

3
DARLENE DIEBLER

When Darlene McIntosh was ten years old, she was so touched by a missionary's speech that she told God she would go wherever He wanted her to. Little did she know just how much following Him would cost her.

Ten years later, she was on her way to New Guinea, an island north of Australia, with five trunks filled with lovely wedding gifts. Darlene and her new husband, Russell Diebler, then made a long, hard journey to the middle of the island to tell the Stone Age cannibals known as Kapaukus about Jesus Christ.

These small, dark-skinned natives had never seen a white woman before. But they liked Darlene instantly, and she loved them back. She and Russell lived in a small house made out of bamboo poles, made friends with the people, and told them about the Lord.

Their time with the Kapaukus was short, however. When World War Two spread and Japan invaded New Guinea, they were forced to move to a nearby island. They worked in a mission Bible school there until it became too dangerous to stay. Then Darlene and Russell had to escape to the mountains with the other missionaries. They were able to take along only a few belongings, and she sadly left behind all her beautiful wedding gifts.

However, the missionaries weren't safe in the mountains, either. Japanese soldiers soon came and took away all the men except Dr. Jaffrey, an elderly man, to a prison camp.

For a year, Darlene and the others that remained were forced to stay where they were. They had little food. She drew strength during this time from Dr. Jaffrey's deep, quiet faith, and she loved him like a father. Then they were all taken to another prison camp that was run by a cruel commander who beat and kicked the women and girls for the smallest reasons. The prisoners worked hard, long days, even though they were fed a poor diet and were often ill.

When the Japanese moved Dr. Jaffrey to a different camp, Darlene wondered what more could be taken away from her. She missed him terribly, but she looked to God for comfort. Everyone in her crowded barracks became a close-knit group after she began leading them in Bible reading and prayer.

The commander saw how the other prisoners loved and respected Darlene, and he put her in charge of her building. Then came the news that Russell had died. By this time, the commander cared about her and tried to comfort her. She told him that she was very sad, but she had hope because she knew Jesus. She told him Jesus had died for him too and that she didn't hate him or any other Japanese people. By the time she finished, the hard-hearted commander had tears running down his cheeks.

Still, things got worse. The secret police accused Darlene of being a spy. They took her to an awful prison where she was beaten and allowed to eat only one cup of rice a day. She became so ill that all of her hair turned white. Finally she was sentenced to die, but her old camp commander convinced higher officials that she was innocent. Just as a guard drew his sword to kill her, some officers drove up to take her back to the old camp.

Once Darlene was back, the commander put her in charge of all the other prisoners. But the prisoners' lives became harder there too. Bombings often forced the women to spend nights in ditches. Their barracks burned, and they had to stay in huts in the jungle. The little they had was gone. Food became even scarcer.

Finally, after Darlene had been in the camp three years, Japan surrendered. She was down to eighty pounds by this time and had to wear borrowed clothes when she was set free.

As she boarded the ship to leave, she vowed never to come back to the islands that had taken so much from her. Only twenty-eight years old, she had lost her husband, her health, and everything she owned. But when she saw the Christian natives running to the shore to say good-bye, she knew she would return someday.

Back home in the United States, Darlene was asked to tell her story in a church. As she finished, she said, "It cost me everything to serve the Lord. For Jesus' sake, I'd do it again."[1]

D I S C U S S

List as many things as you can think of that you have given up or lost for the Lord's sake. What are some things you think He might still want you to give up? Are there any things you would not be willing to lose for Him?

4
DAVE DRAVECKY

BUT ONE THING I DO: FORGETTING WHAT IS BEHIND
AND STRAINING TOWARD WHAT IS AHEAD, I PRESS ON
TOWARD THE GOAL TO WIN THE PRIZE FOR WHICH
GOD HAS CALLED ME HEAVENWARD IN CHRIST
JESUS. (PHILIPPIANS 3:13–14)

Some of Dave Dravecky's happiest childhood memories are of playing Little League baseball with his dad coaching. His whole family loved baseball, so it came as no surprise that Dave dreamed of pitching in the Major Leagues when he grew up.

He played baseball all through high school and college. After graduation, he was drafted into the Minor Leagues—one of the last players picked, because the scouts didn't expect much from him. While he was in the Minors, both he and his wife, Jan, accepted Christ as their personal Savior and found the strength and peace they'd desperately need in the future.

Several coaches told Dave he didn't have enough talent for the big leagues, but his hard work and determination paid off. After five years, he was called up to play for the San Diego Padres as a relief pitcher. Later he made the All-Star team and pitched in the play-offs and the World Series.

In the fall of 1987, Dave noticed a lump on his arm the size of a quarter. The team trainer didn't think it was anything to worry about, and it didn't hurt, so Dave put it out of his mind. By then he was the starting pitcher for the San Francisco Giants, and the National League championship series was about to start.

Dave played the best game of his life during the Giants' second game. With 55,000 fans watching, he gave up only two hits and no runs and put himself in the record books. Afterward, he told reporters that the reason he tried so hard was because he wanted to glorify God.

During the off-season, Dave had tests done on the lump on his arm. The tests didn't reveal any problems, so his doctor told him just to have it checked in another six months.

His pitching was again excellent during the first game of the 1988 season. The Giants won 5 to 1. In the next game, though, his shoulder started hurting whenever he threw hard, and he was put on the disabled list. Surgery on his shoulder didn't seem to help.

By now the lump on his arm had gotten as big as a golf ball, so he had it checked again. Tests this time showed that the lump was a cancerous tumor that would have to be removed. During a thirteen-hour operation, a surgeon cut out half of Dave's deltoid muscle (the one he used to lift his arm and throw) and froze his bone to kill all the cancer attached to it.

When his doctor told him he would never play professional baseball again, Dave said he believed in a God of miracles. If God wanted him to pitch again, he would. If not, He'd have something else for him to do.

No one had ever tried to throw baseballs ninety miles an hour with half a deltoid muscle or after having his bone frozen. But Dave did everything he could to come back and play. He went through months of rough physical therapy before starting grueling workouts with the trainer. Finally, he amazed everyone by pitching again.

During his first game back, the 34,000 fans in the stadium stood and cheered for him twelve times. When he met with reporters after the game, he made clear that God deserved the praise for his amazing comeback.

Dave wasn't able to finish the next game. His arm broke during a pitch, and it broke again two months later. During a checkup, doctors discovered that the cancer was back. He had a second operation to remove the new cancer. Then he was treated with radiation to kill any cancer cells that might still be left.

For the next year and a half, he felt awful. The radiation treatments made him sick. His arm wouldn't heal. It became badly infected and throbbed with pain. He had to take extremely strong antibiotics that made him nauseous.

The tumor came back. Doctors operated a third time. They decided the only way to stop the cancer was to cut off his arm and shoulder. Adjusting to the loss of his arm was hard for Dave. Now, not only could he no longer play baseball, but simple tasks such as tying his shoes and buttoning his clothes suddenly became difficult. He had always prided himself on his independence. Now he had to ask people for help to do things he couldn't do with one arm.

Whenever he was asked how he kept from getting a bitter attitude, he gave God all the credit. He said, "I'm not getting through the loss of my arm because I am a great coper. I'm getting through it because I have a Father in heaven who is a great giver. . . . At the time I need strength, he puts it in my heart or provides it through someone who is close to me."[1]

Dave soon saw that God indeed had other things for him to do. He wrote two books about how the Lord helped his family through their trials, and he began speaking in many places. In time, he and Jan started an organization that helps other families going through troubles.

DISCUSS

When his world fell apart, Dave Dravecky spent little time asking, "Why?" Instead, he asked God, "What next?" Think of some tragedies that could happen to you or your family. How do you think you could cope with them?

5
MARY SLESSOR

So do not fear, for I am with you; do not be
dismayed, for I am your God. I will strengthen
you and help you; I will uphold you with my
righteous right hand. (Isaiah 41:10)

It's been said that brave people aren't those who are fearless but people who take risks even when they're afraid. By that definition, Mary Slessor was truly brave.

Mary was born in 1848 in Scotland. Her mother was a Christian. But her father was an alcoholic, and Mary's life was difficult from the start. He spent his paycheck on his drinking and often beat his wife and children. Sometimes he threw Mary out of the house. The family rarely had enough to eat. Three of Mary's sisters and brothers died. Knowing Jesus helped Mary through all the hard times.

To feed her family, she went to work part-time in a factory when she was eleven years old. By the time she was thirteen, she had quit school and was working from six in the morning until six at night.

As she got older, Mary became very interested in missions. One day a missionary from Calabar, Africa, came to her church. He said Calabar was a land of poisonous swamps, extreme heat, slave trading, disease, murder, and cannibalism. He also said it was ruled by witchcraft, and people were killed as sacrifices to false gods and spirits. In spite of all the dangers, Mary became convinced that God wanted her to go to Calabar as a missionary.

When she was twenty-six, she applied to her church's mission board and was accepted. She studied at a teacher's college and then sailed for Africa. There she learned the language, taught school in a small mission settlement, and began visiting nearby villages.

Back in Scotland, Mary had been a fearful person. Sometimes she wouldn't cross the street alone or walk through a field where a cow was grazing. But in Calabar she often traveled alone through a land full of leopards, poisonous snakes, and crocodiles to tell people about Jesus and nurse the sick. Whenever she became afraid, she reminded herself that God would take care of her.

After a while, she moved farther and farther up the river, where no other missionaries had gone. She went to tribes that were known to be cruel killers. To travel the long distances between villages, she often had to ride in canoes. She was very afraid of them. Sometimes she lay in the bottom of the canoe or sang loudly to keep her mind off her fear. Nights were frightening, too. She slept on the ground or in shacks she made out of branches, twigs, and mud.

Time after time, she showed great bravery in spite of her fears. Because the native people believed that twin babies were evil, they left them in the jungle to die and threw the mother out of the village. Mary risked her own life to rescue the babies and to help their homeless mothers. When the people saw that nothing bad happened to her for doing this, they changed the law to let twins live. She also risked her life many times to save people accused of witchcraft.

During one of her trips up the river, a hippopotamus attacked her canoe. The men rowing the canoe became wild with fear. But Mary grabbed some pots and pans, clanged them together, and hit the hippopotamus with them until it left.

One night she heard screams. She went to investigate and found a woman tied to stakes. A man was getting ready to burn her with boiling oil because she had given some food to a starving slave. Mary rushed between the two and refused to move even though the angry man threatened her. Her bravery caused him to turn away, and she won the people's respect.

Once she received word that a chief from another village was very sick. Her friends told her not to go. If the chief died while she was caring for him, his people would probably kill her. But Mary went.

When she saw the chief, she was worried. Even though she had studied medical books for twelve years, she didn't know what was wrong with him. Then she noticed that his skin was a yellowish color. She gave him aspirin and quinine and prayed and waited. In a few days, he was better, and he asked her to come back and tell his people about the Bible.

The Calabar natives came to love Mary. They called her the White Ma. They built a church and a nice house for her and the children she'd adopted. Because she was so respected, Britain made her a judge of the area (which was under Britain's rule at the time). In 1905, a hospital was built in her name. Mary Slessor was in Africa thirty-six years, until she died of a fever.[1]

DISCUSS

What are some of the things you are most afraid of? How do they affect what you do or don't do? Do you think God wants you to react in some other way to them? Why?

6
GEORGE MULLER

ASK AND IT WILL BE GIVEN TO YOU; SEEK AND YOU
WILL FIND; KNOCK AND THE DOOR WILL BE OPENED
TO YOU. FOR EVERYONE WHO ASKS RECEIVES; HE
WHO SEEKS FINDS; AND TO HIM WHO KNOCKS, THE
DOOR WILL BE OPENED. (MATTHEW 7:7–8)

One of the greatest men of prayer a hundred years ago began as a rebellious troublemaker. George Muller was badly spoiled by his father, who was a rich tax collector in Germany. By the age of ten, he had become a thief, a cheater, and a liar. Again and again he stole the government money that his father collected. By the time he was a teenager, he was also a heavy drinker.

George's father wasn't a Christian, but he wanted George to go to school to become a pastor so that he would have a good job. George said he would, but he didn't do any better. While he was a student, he took a trip and enjoyed himself using money he cheated people out of. He stayed at different expensive hotels and then left without paying. All seemed to go his way until he got caught sneaking out of a window and was put in jail.

George was in jail for several weeks before his father paid his debts and he was set free. This bad experience caused him to work harder at his studies, but it didn't change his wild ways.

Then one day George went to a prayer meeting with some Christians and realized what he'd been missing. He asked Christ to come into his heart, and his life was never again the same. From then on, whenever he was asked to preach, he spoke with a heart filled with love.

He finished school and moved to England. There he married a godly woman and became the pastor of a tiny church. George believed that he should trust God to provide what they needed, so he told his people they did not have to pay him a certain salary. Instead, he suggested that a box be left in the church and whoever wanted to leave a gift for him could do so.

Over the next few years, there were many times when he and his wife did not know how they would pay the rent or buy food. But they saw God answer prayers and supply what they needed again and again. God used that time to help them learn to trust Him more.

George was soon asked to come to a larger church in Bristol, but God was working in him to start a new work. One day the verse in Psalm 68 that says God is "a father to the fatherless" spoke to him. If God provides for the fatherless, he thought, then all he had to do to help them was be the man God used to meet their needs.

Later, he read about a man in Germany named August Franke, who had trusted God to help him care for nearly two thousand orphans. Inspired by his example, George started a Christian school for orphans and street children. Shortly after that, he started an orphanage too. Within a few years, his orphanage was caring for nearly one hundred children. Many times the orphanage had little or no money left, but George never went out asking for money. Instead, he prayed and trusted God to provide. And God always did.

One day the children were at the table waiting to eat. Knowing they had no food in the house, he prayed and thanked God for the food they were about to receive. Soon a baker came to the door. He had gotten up in the middle of the night to bake them some bread, because the Lord told him they didn't have any. Then there was another knock at the door. It was a milkman. His cart had broken down in front of the orphanage. He gave them all of his milk so that he could get the cart fixed.

George often spent two or three hours each day on his knees praying or walking back and forth in his study, praising God and asking Him to supply the orphans' needs.

As God answered his prayers, he had faith to ask for more things. In time, the orphanage was caring for 2,000 children. During his lifetime, George's prayers brought in more than $7.5 million to carry on his ministry to the orphans. Eventually his work would expand to send out 189 missionaries, support around one hundred schools, and distribute thousands of Bibles and millions of leaflets explaining the gospel. Near the end of his life, this wonderful man of prayer said he had read the Bible through about two hundred times. Half of those times, he was on his knees as he read.

Discuss

Who is the first person you usually go to when you have a problem or need help? Why? Have you ever had a need and not told anyone except God about it? Why do you think George Muller did that? Can you think of some times when it would be better not to talk with other people about a need or problem?

7
MICHELLE PRICE

A CHEERFUL HEART IS GOOD MEDICINE, BUT A
CRUSHED SPIRIT DRIES UP THE BONES. (PROVERBS 17:22)

Michelle Price was a lively little girl who climbed trees, rode horses, skied, told far-out stories, and sang a lot. With a loving Christian family, her life was carefree until she was eight
years old. That's when her right leg became swollen and started to hurt.

After the doctor ran tests, he told Michelle's parents she had a very deadly kind of bone
cancer. He said her chances of living were less than 4 percent and that most of her leg would
have to be removed right away.

Her parents dreaded telling Michelle. When they did, at first she said, "Oh, Daddy, I won't
be able to dance anymore if I don't have my leg! I don't want to be a cripple." She sobbed for
a few minutes. But then she saw her mother's tear-streaked face. She stopped crying, took a
deep breath, and said, "I'm going to be OK, Mommy. Don't cry anymore." Patting her mother's face, she went on, "I was scared when Daddy told me, but Jesus made me feel safe inside.
I'm going to be all right. You'll see."

She calmly asked her father why God had let this happen. When he said he didn't know,
Michelle thought for a few minutes before speaking again. "Maybe I know," she said. "If they
don't have any medicine to fix this kind of sickness yet, maybe they can study my leg and find
some. Then they can help other kids when they get sick."[1]

The doctors removed Michelle's leg four to five inches above the knee. She cried when
she first looked at the bandaged leg. Then she told her mom how frightened she had been
before going to sleep in the operating room—until she remembered she wasn't alone. Jesus
was there with her.

Michelle had intense phantom pains for a while. The nerve endings in the leg that was
gone kept telling her brain that something was wrong, causing pain. Yet, three days after her
surgery, she surprised her doctor by joking about her stump and drawing a happy face on the
bandages. The doctor told her parents that it normally took weeks before most amputees
could make themselves even look at their missing part.

Five days after the surgery, the doctors started giving Michelle chemotherapy—powerful
drugs designed to kill cancer cells. Because the cancer she had was so deadly, they gave her a
dose a thousand times greater than usual.

Soon the drugs made all of her hair fall out. Each treatment made her extremely sick. She
vomited and got such bad chills that her body shook the bed. But whenever anyone came in

and asked how she was feeling, she said, "Doing OK," so she wouldn't make anyone else feel bad.

After four weeks in the hospital, she was allowed to go home for a few days. When she went out with her dad, she realized the neighbors were uncomfortable around her because of her leg and her bald head. To make them feel better, she went to each neighbor's home, told them about her cancer, and invited them to ask questions.

Michelle had chemotherapy off and on for eighteen months and showed great bravery through all of the pain and discomfort. When she felt better, she visited other children in the hospital who had cancer and tried to cheer them up. Then tests showed that her own cancer hadn't come back, and Michelle was filled with thankfulness.

In time, she learned to ski with one leg and ride a skateboard and play soccer using crutches. After she won several medals at a national skiing contest for handicapped people, Wayne Newton gave her on national television a special sports award for courage. When Mr. Newton saw how she spent her time trying to make others happy, he became very fond of her and surprised her with a special birthday present—her own horse.

Michelle once told her mom she sometimes felt bad when she was picked last for sports or when she wondered if boys would like her with just one leg. Then she added, "I feel bad about feeling bad. God's gonna think I'm not grateful for what He's done. I think I'm looking at the bad too much, and not enough at what's good."[2]

As she got older, Michelle became the youngest world-class handicapped skier, a fashion model, an inspirational speaker, and one of the top disabled horse-riders in the country. She went to college and afterward worked in a center that helps people who have lost an arm or leg. In 1993, she was given an award for courage by the American Cancer Society.

Now Michelle is a young wife and mother. She dreams of someday starting a camp for disabled kids to help give them a positive attitude.

DISCUSS

How did Michelle's attitude affect her friends and family? How could her example help strangers? How did it honor God? Have you ever known anyone with a big problem who still had a positive attitude? Who? How did that person affect you?

8

BROTHER ANDREW

"BECAUSE HE LOVES ME," SAYS THE LORD, "I WILL
RESCUE HIM; I WILL PROTECT HIM, FOR HE
ACKNOWLEDGES MY NAME. HE WILL CALL UPON ME,
AND I WILL ANSWER HIM; I WILL BE WITH HIM IN
TROUBLE, I WILL DELIVER HIM AND HONOR HIM."

(PSALM 91:14–15)

Brother Andrew (a name he uses to hide who he really is) grew up in a small Dutch village with five sisters and brothers, a hardworking father, and a loving Christian mother. In spite of his mother's prayers, the boy Andrew wasn't interested in God. When his brother died, he became angry with God and turned away from Him even more. It was after he joined the army and was wounded in battle that his mother's prayers were finally answered. Then he not only trusted Christ, but he also decided to become a missionary.

In 1955, Andrew was finishing his schooling when he saw a magazine article about a Communist youth festival that would take place that summer in Poland. Knowing that thousands of young people from all over the world would be there, he went, too. He took with him a suitcase full of booklets explaining salvation in every European language.

While he was there, he handed out the booklets and talked to Polish Christians to see how much freedom they really had. They told him the Communists were trying to stamp out Christianity so that the government would be the most important thing in people's lives. Bibles were very scarce. No one was allowed to print them or bring them into the country. Christians were often threatened, put in jail, and abused.

Later, Andrew went to Czechoslovakia on a tour. It was run by Communists, who wanted to show only the good side of life under Communism. He broke away from the tour and visited church services. He saw many people writing the words to hymns and Bible verses in notebooks so that they could have their own copies.

He wanted to help these struggling Christians, but he knew it would be extremely dangerous and lonely work. At the time, there wasn't a single missionary who dared to work in the Communist countries of the Soviet Union.

Back home again, Andrew applied for visas—written permission—to enter other Communist lands. Every time he listed his occupation as "Missionary" he was turned down. The Communists didn't want religious people coming into their countries. He didn't know what to do. He didn't want to lie. Then he remembered that he was also a teacher. When he wrote that on his application, he got a visa to go to Yugoslavia.

God supplied what he needed to go. People who read the articles he wrote about his trips and the work he hoped to do began sending him money. He had never owned a car. Now a Christian friend gave him a blue Volkswagen.

As Andrew got close to Yugoslavia, he knew he would need God's help more than ever. The guards at the border would surely search his car. If they saw the Christian leaflets and Bibles, they would take them and probably put him in jail. Being arrested in a Communist country was not like being arrested in the United States; there was no guarantee that he'd be treated fairly. He prayed that God would somehow keep the guards from seeing the Christian literature.

When he stopped at the border, one guard poked around his sleeping bag and tent but didn't notice the boxes of Christian leaflets that were hidden in them. The other guard opened a suitcase and lifted the shirts on top. This left a pile of leaflets in plain sight. But when Andrew started talking, the guard became distracted. Without looking back at the suitcase, he nodded that Andrew could close it. Andrew stayed in Yugoslavia seven weeks—preaching, teaching, and giving out Bibles.

After he married and had children, it became harder for him to take the risks involved in his work, but he saw God's protection again and again. Once, when entering Romania, he watched six cars ahead of him undergo long, thorough inspections—a half hour to an hour each. But when the guard came to Andrew's car (full of Romanian Bibles), he leaned against the door, looked at Andrew's passport, and waved him through. In Hungary, he was taken in for questioning after being caught preaching, but he was released.

Seeing how much he could help made the danger and time away from his family worth it all. In Moscow, he met the pastor of a large church who didn't even own a Bible. When Andrew gave him one, the man hugged him until Andrew's chest hurt. In Bulgaria, he met a couple who had spent a month's income to buy part of a Bible. Later he met a man who had traveled 2,000 miles after being told in a dream he'd find a Bible in the city where Andrew was. He was often moved to tears by the people's joy and gratitude when he gave them God's Word.

Others began to work with Andrew, and his ministry spread throughout Asia, Africa, Central America, and the Middle East. In 1981, Brother Andrew and his workers secretly brought one million Bibles into Communist China. Each step of the way, he has felt God's blessing and protection.

DISCUSS

Describe the riskiest thing you've ever done. Do you think it was a risk God wanted you to take? What are some risks you think He might ask you to take in the future?

9
JONI EARECKSON TADA

THEREFORE WE DO NOT LOSE HEART. THOUGH
OUTWARDLY WE ARE WASTING AWAY, YET INWARDLY
WE ARE BEING RENEWED DAY BY DAY. FOR OUR
LIGHT AND MOMENTARY TROUBLES ARE ACHIEVING
FOR US AN ETERNAL GLORY THAT FAR OUTWEIGHS
THEM ALL. SO WE FIX OUR EYES NOT ON WHAT IS
SEEN, BUT ON WHAT IS UNSEEN. FOR WHAT IS SEEN IS
TEMPORARY, BUT WHAT IS UNSEEN IS ETERNAL.

(2 CORINTHIANS 4:16–18)

Joni Eareckson grew up in an active family that often swam, hiked, and went backpacking together. Her father taught her to ride horses; her mother taught her to play tennis. When she got older, she played hockey and became the captain of her high school lacrosse team. She won many ribbons doing trick riding with her horse. But all that changed on July 30, 1967, when Joni was seventeen.

While diving into Chesapeake Bay, she hit a rock, which crushed her spine. When she was pulled out of the water, she couldn't move her arms and legs or feel anything below her shoulders.

In the hospital, doctors drilled holes into the sides of her head, put in metal tongs, and attached cables to keep her head from moving. Lying flat on her back, she was put in a sandwichlike canvas and metal frame so that she could be flipped over every two hours. First she stared at the ceiling; then the whole frame was turned upside down and she faced the floor.

The next weeks were terrifying. Joni's doctors weren't sure she would live. She couldn't eat without getting sick, so she was fed through a tube into her veins. Her weight dropped to eighty pounds. Heavy doses of medicine gave her hallucinations like nightmares. The one thing that kept her going was believing she would get better. When her doctor finally told her she would be paralyzed permanently, she became so depressed that she wanted to die.

As her friends left for college, Joni began painful physical therapy sessions to train the muscles she could still use to do extra work for some she could no longer control. After three and one-half months in the hospital, she was moved to a rehabilitation center where she learned to live with her paralysis. Because she had been lying flat for so long, she was gradually tilted a few minutes at a time until she could finally be raised to a sitting position. Later, she learned to draw and paint, holding pencils and brushes with her teeth.

Joni was at the first center a year. Then she went to another, where she learned to use a wheelchair and was fitted for arm braces. After working very hard, she finally learned to feed herself. She used a spoon attached to her brace and swung her arm, using shoulder muscles. At last she was ready to leave, and she went to live with her sister, Jay.

Joni was a Christian, but that didn't keep her from struggling spiritually during the years following her accident. She couldn't understand why God didn't answer all of her family's, her friends', and her own prayers for healing.

Along the way, a new friend named Steve Estes came into her life. He held a weekly Bible study in Jay's home and encouraged Joni in many ways. As she spent more time studying the Bible and praying, she began to accept God's will and learned to praise Him in spite of her circumstances or feelings. Steve persuaded her to start telling her story to church groups and to take speech classes at a nearby college.

In the meantime, a man saw one of her drawings in her father's office, and he arranged an art show for her. When word got out that she did all of her artwork using her mouth, she was interviewed on local and national television shows. Soon she was getting many invitations to be in art shows and to speak to different groups. She wrote a book about her experiences and even played herself in a movie made about her life and her faith in God.

After the movie was finished, Joni prayed about what God wanted her to do next. She realized that many disabled people didn't have loving family and friends as she did, and she decided to start a ministry in California to help them. Her organization, Joni and Friends, encourages handicapped people and helps them in many practical ways. And Joni found more than work to do in California; she also met a handsome teacher named Ken Tada. Eventually he became her husband.

It's been more than thirty years since Joni's accident. Her trust in God has deepened with each year, but life is still and always will be difficult for her. Every morning, someone has to get her out of bed, dress her, and fix her breakfast. Nearly every night she has to go to bed at 8:00 because of her physical condition.

The thought of another thirty years in a wheelchair could easily overwhelm her. But Joni chooses to take one day at a time, to praise God in spite of her troubles, and to live in the power of His Spirit. Her obedient attitude and determination to choose joy have inspired thousands through the books she has written, her daily radio program, and the songs she has recorded.

DISCUSS

Have you ever prayed for something really important to you and had God say, "No," or, "Not yet"? Or have you gone through some trouble you couldn't see a reason for? What was your reaction?

10
ERIC LIDDELL

TEACH ME TO DO YOUR WILL, FOR YOU ARE MY
GOD; MAY YOUR GOOD SPIRIT LEAD ME ON LEVEL
GROUND. (PSALM 143:10)

He was one of Scotland's most beloved athletes, but Eric Liddell became better known for what he didn't do than for what he did.

Eric was born in China to missionary parents. When he and his brother were old enough, they were sent to boarding school (a school that students live in) in Scotland. He became a fine athlete and a champion at rugby, a game like football. He also set a school record in the one-hundred-yard dash.

When he went on to the university, Eric played rugby in international contests. He also ran races and began training two or three times a week. Soon he was winning one trophy after another in national and international meets.

After becoming the British champion in the one-hundred-meter sprint, he planned to run it in the 1924 Olympics. This was considered one of the most important races, and Eric was expected to win the gold medal. But when he heard that the race would be held on a Sunday, he said he wouldn't compete. He believed Sunday should be a day to rest and focus on the Lord.

His decision was reported around the world. Many people thought he was letting his country down. Even though he was pressured to change his mind, he quietly refused. If he could not run and honor God, he would not run.

Although there wasn't much time left before the Olympics, he began training for the quarter-mile race. That would not be held on a Sunday. On the day of that race, someone slipped him a note that said, "In the old book it says, 'He that honours me, I will honour.'"[1]

God did honor Eric for his obedience. He not only won the quarter-mile race, but he also set a world's record. When he came home with a gold medal, even those who had criticized him considered him a national hero.

While he finished college, he was in great demand to speak at gospel meetings. His tremendous popularity drew large crowds, and his words and his life caused many to trust in Christ. But Eric didn't believe this kind of speaking was God's plan for his life. After he graduated, he left Scotland, his fame, his adoring fans, and a stream of job offers. He traded it all for a life of hardship in a country where foreigners were often mistreated. He went back to China and taught science in a mission school.

While he was teaching there, he fell in love with the daughter of other missionaries. Eric and Florence were married and soon had two little girls whom he adored.

They had a very happy home until he was asked to work in the war-torn countryside. China was in the middle of a civil war. At the same time, Japan had invaded the country and was taking over more and more territory. Because of the danger, Eric's family would have to stay in the city. He hated the idea of being away from his wife and girls for long periods of time, but he believed God wanted him to say yes.

He became a traveling preacher, making long journeys on foot or by bicycle, dodging bandits and soldiers as he went. He loved people. He was friendly to everyone and won many friends. His tender heart compelled him to rescue wounded soldiers from every army. This was extremely risky, because the Japanese killed anyone they caught helping Chinese soldiers.

Then Britain declared war on Japan, and it became especially dangerous for British citizens to remain in China. Eric sent his wife and two daughters to Canada for their safety. He never saw them again.

Less than two years later, all foreigners still in the country were rounded up and taken to prison camps. Many different kinds of people were crowded together. In the summer, the heat was unbearable. There wasn't enough food. The stress caused some to have mental breakdowns.

Although Eric missed his own family terribly, he kept busy trying to cheer up everyone else. When tempers flared, he was the peacemaker. When others were too weak to do their work, he did it on top of his own. When the camp's children were bored, he taught them math and science and arranged sports activities.

But after eighteen months in the prison camp, Eric became weak and exhausted. He began having terrible headaches. Within a short time, he died of a brain tumor. The entire camp was stunned by his death, because he was so greatly loved.

DISCUSS

Throughout his life, Eric Liddell asked himself, "Does this path I [walk] follow the Lord's will?"[2] How can we know whether or not our plans are God's will for our lives?

11
JOHN PERKINS

YOU HAVE HEARD THAT IT WAS SAID, "LOVE YOUR NEIGHBOR AND HATE YOUR ENEMY." BUT I TELL YOU: LOVE YOUR ENEMIES AND PRAY FOR THOSE WHO PERSECUTE YOU, THAT YOU MAY BE SONS OF YOUR FATHER IN HEAVEN. (MATTHEW 5:43–45)

John Perkins was only four years old when he started working all day long picking cotton. His mother had died when he was a baby, and his father left John and his older brother, Clyde. So John and Clyde lived with their grandmother, aunts, uncles, and cousins.

Like many other blacks in Mississippi in the 1930s, John's family were sharecroppers. That meant they farmed land that was part of a large plantation. The owner required them to give him half of what they made farming and to buy their supplies from his expensive store—where he charged 30 to 45 percent interest on the money they owed. No matter how hard John's family worked, they were always in debt to the owner.

John and his cousins went to school only three or four months a year. They had to work in the fields the rest of the time. So it took them two or three years to finish one grade. Every school day, they walked five miles to their three-room schoolhouse.

On John's first day of school, his cousin pulled him to the side of the road when a yellow school bus came toward them. As the bus passed, a white boy inside yelled, "Move off the road!" and called John an ugly name. Someone else threw a large rock that hit him on the arm and left a bruise.

John didn't understand. The white children went to a different school. They had a school bus. They didn't have to walk for miles the way black children did. Why did they hate him?

Before he reached the fourth grade, World War Two started. Clyde and John's older cousins left to join the army. John was needed in the fields full-time, so he dropped out of school and never returned.

Clyde was wounded several times in Germany. The army gave him a Purple Heart medal and sent him home to Mississippi. But he didn't get a hero's welcome. Instead, a sheriff who hated black people shot Clyde as he stood outside a movie theater. Clyde died several hours later. John burned with anger.

John's family believed that his life would also be in danger if he stayed, so they sent him to California with three dollars in his pocket. He soon found a job in a factory that paid many times what he had made in Mississippi.

In California his life was better in many ways. In the South he was very limited as to what he could do and where he could go because of the color of his skin. In California, he worked alongside whites and was treated as an equal. He was free to go wherever he wanted to go.

Later, John was drafted into the army and married a pretty girl named Vera. When he was finished serving his time in the military, he got a job as a janitor. But with hard work and a sharp mind, John quickly moved up in the company. Soon he had enough money to buy a nice big house. Still, he felt something was missing.

John found the peace and joy he'd been looking for when his little boy asked him to go to church. He gave his life to the Lord and began studying the Bible. He also gave his testimony at businessmen's meetings, and he and Vera taught the children in their neighborhood about Jesus.

After a while, he felt that God wanted him to go back to Mississippi and help black people there build better lives. His relatives thought he was crazy to trade his happy, secure life in California for hardship in the South. But he and Vera set out with their five children and a trailer of belongings.

Two California churches promised to send seventy-five dollars a month for the Perkins family to live on. John chopped wood and picked cotton to earn the rest while he preached, taught Bible schools, and led many kids to Christ. Eventually, he started an organization that built a playground and gym and started a tutoring program, a cooperative food store, a day care, and a health center.

Things went fairly smoothly until John started helping blacks register to vote so they'd be able to change some of the things that were wrong in the South. Then he received many threats, and men with guns began sitting in cars near his house.

The trouble between blacks and whites grew worse. One day he heard that police had arrested a busload of black students who were coming back from a peaceful protest march. John and a couple friends went to the police station to try to help them.

When they got there, John himself was arrested and badly beaten. Later, as he lay bleeding in the jail, he felt pity for the men who had battered him, because their hearts were filled with hate. He asked God to fill him with love for them. But the beating and the stress he'd been under took a toll on John's health. Within five months, he had a heart attack. Not long after that, he was hospitalized with severe ulcers, and two-thirds of his stomach had to be removed.

John still refused to hate back. Instead, he started ministries to black people in other cities. He traveled about the United States, telling people of the healing power of God's love. In 1989, he organized the Christian Community Development Association, which has grown to more than three hundred ministries across the country.

DISCUSS

Have you ever been tempted to hate someone? How did you overcome your feelings? How do we hurt ourselves more than anyone else when we give in to hate?

12

SUSANNA WESLEY

DEVOTE YOURSELVES TO PRAYER, BEING WATCHFUL
AND THANKFUL. (COLOSSIANS 4:2)

It would be an understatement to say Susanna Annesley came from a large family. She was the twenty-fifth child of a well-known London minister. She was also an intelligent, deeply spiritual girl. Susanna's daily prayer was "Dear God, guide me. Help me do Thy will. Make my life count."[1]

Susanna lived in fear that her father would be arrested for his preaching. He was a preacher in the Dissenters' church. The Dissenters were Christians who worshiped God in their own way rather than following the rules of the Church of England. In the late 1600s it was against the law to preach for any church other than the Church of England. Dissenters had been branded, had their ears cut off, and been burned alive. Once, soldiers came to the Annesley home and took many of their belongings as a fine because of her father's preaching.

Susanna dearly loved and respected her father. From him she learned to study and pray at the same time every day—a habit she would one day teach her own children.

When she was nineteen, Susanna married Samuel Wesley. Samuel was not only a very committed minister, but he too was highly intelligent and well educated. He also loved to write. Unfortunately for Susanna, he was not a practical man.

Their first home was drab and tiny. Samuel's job at a small church in a village near London paid very little. They soon had a baby boy and named him Samuel after his father. Susanna prayed that God would use their son and the children that would come later to make a difference in the world.

After a few years, Samuel got a job in a bigger church in the country, one hundred miles from London. Although his pay was better and a house was provided for them, the move was difficult for Susanna. One hundred miles was a long way to be separated from family and friends when the only means of travel was by horse and carriage. She might never see them again.

Samuel spent most of his free time writing magazine articles and poetry, so it was up to Susanna to see that their growing family was clothed and fed. But in spite of Samuel's shortcomings, Susanna loved him.

Her strong faith saw her through many hardships. Three of their first seven children died. Her oldest son had never talked. On top of that, Samuel made an important man angry by telling the woman he was living with that what they were doing was sinful. This meant he was sure to lose his job.

During those dark days, Susanna turned to God for help. She was given a ray of joy when little Samuel finally began to talk when he was five years old. She began teaching him to read and found he had a very quick mind and memorized easily.

Then her husband was offered a job in another town. It paid better still, and a big house on three acres of land was included. Now they could grow their own food. But there were moving expenses. Their growing family needed more furniture. They also needed to buy equipment and animals before they could do any farming. All of this put them in debt equal to a year's salary.

The unschooled church people in the new place didn't get along well with the Wesleys, who were educated and had famous and important ancestors. They also didn't like Samuel's political ideas and his loyalty to the king. A lonely Susanna turned to God for comfort.

One time while Samuel was away, the family was kept awake by gunshots and an angry mob's pounding and shouting. Because Susanna was recovering from giving birth, a nurse was taking care of her baby across the street. When the mob finally left, the tired nurse fell into a deep sleep and rolled over on the baby and smothered it.

Some time later, an angry church member demanded that Samuel pay him some money he owed him right away. Samuel couldn't, so the man had him put into prison for three months. While he was gone, one of his enemies killed all their cows, Susanna's main means of support. Friends helped her and paid Samuel's debt.

In 1702, a fire ruined two-thirds of their home. Rebuilding the house put them deeper in debt. Seven years later, another fire destroyed nearly everything they owned.

As if constant money troubles and problems with the townspeople weren't enough, seven more of Susanna's children died. Of their nineteen children, only nine lived to be adults.

Through it all, Susanna spent six hours a day teaching them. Determined that her children would learn their duty toward God and their neighbors, she wrote three religious textbooks for them. Her teaching was so effective that every one of them grew to love learning and godly living. Somehow, Susanna managed to spend two hours a day in her own Bible reading and prayer.

In the end, Susanna's teaching, her daily prayers for her children, and her own godly example made a great impact on her world. While her sons John and Charles were studying at college, they started a club with other students who wanted to know and serve God better. The group became known as Methodists, because they had methods for praying, fasting, and studying the Bible at set times.

Later, tens of thousands would hear John and Charles. John led the Methodist revival in England, which turned people back to the true gospel. And Charles carried the message to countless churches through the hymns he wrote.

DISCUSS

It's been said that God is always waiting to speak to us. Do you make an appointment to meet Him each day? How often do you keep Him waiting?

13

FRANKLIN GRAHAM

FOR GOD DID NOT GIVE US A SPIRIT OF TIMIDITY,
BUT A SPIRIT OF POWER, OF LOVE AND OF
SELF-DISCIPLINE. (2 TIMOTHY 1:7)

Many people expected Franklin to walk in his father's footsteps, but when your father is Billy Graham, those footsteps look awfully big. And Franklin Graham, Billy's oldest son, wanted to make his own way.

Franklin was a strong-willed child. He was willing to risk punishment to do anything he really wanted to do—such as smoke cigarettes and tease his sisters mercilessly. It didn't make things any easier to have so many people expecting him to behave perfectly because of who his father was.

He loved adventure and the outdoors. Some of his happiest times were spent hunting, hiking, and camping in the North Carolina hills, especially when his father was with him. He hated being cooped up in school. He hated studying subjects that didn't interest him. His grades often showed it.

When Franklin was thirteen, his parents thought it would help to send him to a Christian boarding school in New York. He hated that too. He was required to wear a suit or blazer and a tie to class every day. The other students made fun of his Southern accent. He desperately missed his home, his freedom, his family, and the North Carolina hills. During the first two months, he would quietly cry himself to sleep.

He made friends with other students who also didn't want to be there. They broke school rules. They sneaked in cigarettes and beer whenever they could get by with it. Part of Franklin wanted to get expelled, but the other part didn't want to disappoint his parents or make his father look bad. By his junior year, though, he knew his days were just about up. He asked his parents to let him come back home before he was kicked out. They agreed.

Even though Franklin was thrilled to be home, he still couldn't manage to stay out of trouble. He got into a few fights at school, and he couldn't resist speeding in front of their small-town policeman—until his father put his foot down.

He loved noise, speed, and smoke. So it was only natural that he loved motorcycles. When he was eleven, he had done odd jobs and bought a minibike, and he graduated to bigger bikes when he was older. While he was in college in Texas, he learned to fly an airplane—although not without crash-landing once along the way.

Then his father arranged for a summer job where Franklin made travel arrangements for a Bible tour to the Middle East. While in Jordan, he met two missionary women who ran a hospital there. They told him they needed a better vehicle and that they were building a new hospital so they could help more people.

Ever ready for an adventure, Franklin came up with a plan. He asked his father if the Billy Graham Evangelistic Association would buy the women a Land Rover. Then he and his college roommate would take a semester off to personally deliver it and help build the hospital. Billy agreed but said he would have to pay his own way. To raise the money, Franklin reluctantly decided to sell his most prized possession—his car.

It was at the height of the Cold War just then—a time when Russia was trying to take over parts of the world—so they had trouble crossing borders from one country to another. But the time Franklin spent in Jordan made a lasting impact on his life. The way the missionaries trusted God to provide their needs deeply touched him. He also enjoyed knowing he was helping.

He still wasn't ready to give his life to the Lord, though. He thought Christianity would be boring—it would just be more living by other people's rules. He wanted to live "hard, fast, and free, to experience life on the edge."[1]

His first semester back in college, he was expelled for breaking a rule. He started attending a local college, determined to work hard and stay out of trouble this time. But he still wanted to help those missionaries in Jordan. His father introduced him to people interested in missions, including a man named Bob Pierce. Bob had started a Christian relief organization called Samaritan's Purse. He raised thousands of dollars for the Jordan hospital and became Franklin's friend.

When Franklin was twenty-two, he realized he was tired of running from God and gave his life to Him. A short time later, he asked a hometown girl to marry him. Jane Austin had trusted Christ a few months before. They were married and attended a Bible college in Colorado.

While Franklin was wondering what God wanted him to do next, Bob Pierce called and asked him to travel with him for a few months. They visited several different countries where people were in need. He challenged Franklin to commit himself to bigger things than he could do by himself and then watch God work a miracle. Bob also told him about his health problem—Bob had leukemia, cancer of the blood. He would not live long.

In the spring of 1978, two local surgeons asked Franklin to help them. They wanted to send Christian doctors to missionary hospitals around the world for short-term service. Franklin wrote all the mission organizations with hospitals to see if there was a need for such a ministry. The response was overwhelmingly positive, so he agreed to start and run World Medical Mission.

Bob Pierce asked him to take over the work of Samaritan's Purse after he died. By the time the organization's board of directors offered Franklin the job, he knew it was God's will. The board agreed to bring Samaritan's Purse and World Medical Mission together.

This work has provided more than enough excitement to satisfy Franklin Graham's sense of adventure. He has personally traveled through war zones—dodging bullets and exploding rockets—to survey situations before Samaritan's Purse got involved.

The organization provides food, supplies, blankets, clothing, and medicine. Sometimes it helps build churches, hospitals, schools, and homes for children. At other times it digs wells and provides seed, farming equipment, or milk cows. In some countries it replaces windows broken by gunfire and buys stoves to heat homes. Around Christmas, it distributes more than a million shoe boxes filled with gifts to needy children in different parts of the world. And while responding to physical needs, Samaritan's Purse always shares the gospel.

When Franklin was younger, the thought of preaching at a crusade and being compared to his incredible father sent shivers down his spine. But in the late 1980s, he realized that God was also calling him to evangelism. He became an associate evangelist with the Billy Graham Evangelistic Association. He has recently been named as the person who will take his father's place when Billy can no longer preach.

Between trips around the globe, Franklin returns to his forty-acre farm in North Carolina, to his wife and four children, a host of barnyard animals, and a barn filled with motorcycles, a tractor, and a fishing boat. Undoubtedly a big grin crosses his face whenever he remembers his fears that being a Christian would be boring.

D ISCUSS

Is the Christian life an adventure to you? Why or why not? Do you know someone who "lives on the edge" for Christ?

14

GLADYS AYLWARD

WHEN I CALLED, YOU ANSWERED ME; YOU MADE ME
BOLD AND STOUTHEARTED. (PSALM 138:3)

Gladys Aylward was working as a maid in London when she became convinced that God wanted her to become a missionary to China. At the age of twenty-six, she went to the China Inland Mission training school. But after three months, the principal told her she wasn't doing well enough in her classes. He didn't think she'd ever be able to learn the difficult Chinese language.

Although she was slender and only five feet tall, Gladys had a tremendous amount of determination. She was still convinced that God wanted her to go to China, and she decided to go on her own. She worked hard and saved her money and was thrilled to hear that a seventy-three-year-old missionary in China was looking for a younger woman to help her.

The missionary, Jeannie Lawson, told Gladys she could join her if she could just get to Tientsin, a large city in northeast China. From there a guide would take her the rest of the way. Gladys set out in October of 1930. A war going on between Russia and China made her journey long and dangerous.

She had to take many detours before she finally found Jeannie, living in a large, run-down building in a wild, mountainous area. Since the people in this remote region believed all foreigners were devils, they threw dried mud and spat at the two women and slammed doors in their faces.

The ladies decided to turn their home into an inn for the men who sold goods from town to town. They planned to tell them Bible stories so that the gospel would spread hundreds of miles as the men traveled.

But how would they get the men to stop? They were afraid of the "foreign devils." Gladys and Jeannie decided that Gladys would pull the men's mules into the courtyard. Once there, they thought, the tired mules would refuse to move. Their plan worked. After the men got over their fear of them, they came regularly to the Inn of Six Happinesses. This helped the neighbors become friendlier. Soon they were willing to listen to Bible stories, too.

And Gladys did learn to speak Chinese. She also learned five different dialects (kinds of Chinese languages). When Jeannie died, Gladys worked on.

One time she was asked to come to the men's prison during a riot. The governor of the prison told her that the convicts were killing each other and the soldiers were afraid to go inside. He wanted her to go in because she had told everyone she had the living God inside her and He protected her. Although she was terrified, Gladys knew that no one would believe her message if she refused.

Inside the jail, it looked and sounded as if the criminals had gone insane. There were bodies lying on the ground and blood everywhere. A convict came running at her, swinging a large ax. Gladys told him to give her the ax. This took him so by surprise that he handed it to her. Seeing this, the other prisoners stopped what they were doing and stared.

Gladys asked why they were acting that way. They said they were starving and had nothing to do day after day. She convinced the governor to give them work and a chance to make money to buy food. After that, she often visited the grateful prisoners and told them about Jesus.

Japan invaded China in 1937 and soon took over all of the northeastern part of the country. By 1938, Gladys's mission was nearly destroyed by bombs, but she stayed and cared for hundreds of wounded people, orphans, and refugees.

To escape the Japanese, the Chinese people fled to the hills and mountains where they lived in remote villages and even caves. Gladys moved on to other Christian missions to help with the orphans. At one place, soldiers knocked her down and kicked her until she was unconscious.

Because Japanese soldiers were killing so many Chinese, she began giving important information to the Chinese troops so they could defend their country. As soon as the Japanese found out, they considered Gladys a spy and offered a large reward for her capture.

Gladys believed that the Japanese soldiers would probably kill the two hundred orphans at a certain mission station if they weren't moved. Then she heard that a government agency would take care of them if they could be brought to Sian. Gladys immediately sent one hundred children to Sian with a Chinese Christian, along with money and supplies. They arrived safely in five weeks. Gladys planned to send the rest of the children when the man came back, but he was arrested on the way. It would be up to Gladys now—and there was a reward for her capture.

Gladys moved the children back to the Inn of Six Happinesses. But she was forced to flee when soldiers fired on her. A bullet grazed her back, and she narrowly escaped by crawling into a moat. She later made her way back to the inn and set off the next day with one hundred children, aged four to fifteen.

They had to cross through dangerous Japanese territory, so they stayed away from known trails. Much of the time they were in country Gladys had never been in before. They had no money. They had no food except for two baskets of grain, and those were soon gone. Gladys sent the older boys into deserted villages to look for scraps of food. Sometimes Chinese soldiers gave them some. Gladys always ate last. Often there was little food left, so she went without.

Occasionally they slept in remote villages. Usually they slept outside. They wore thin, homemade cloth shoes that had bark on the bottom. The shoes soon wore out, leaving their feet cut and blistered. The sun beat down on them as they climbed one steep mountain after another. Gladys and the older boys took turns carrying the smaller children. She felt weak and sick during the whole journey, but she pushed on for the children's sake.

They finally got to a town beside the Yellow River, but only one man was there. Everyone had left because the Japanese army was coming. There was no way to get across the deep, swift river. All the boats had been moved to the other side to slow down the Japanese. For three days Gladys and the children waited and prayed at the edge of the river, wondering how soon the Japanese soldiers would get there. On the fourth day, a Chinese soldier who was out scouting saw them and got them a boat. It took three trips to carry them all across.

They traveled a few more days. Then an official arranged for them to ride a train for four days. When they got off the train, they still had several days of travel left through high mountains. They had been on the road for weeks now, soaked by rains and chilled by winds. They had gone without food and had hardly slept. At one point they all cried from exhaustion until Gladys picked herself up and told the children they would sing a hymn as they marched.

Next, they got on a freight train, where the children were wedged into piles of coal to keep from falling off. They rode to a town that had a refugee center, and there people arranged for them to take another train to Sian.

But when they got to Sian, they were told that the city gates were closed. No more refugees were allowed in. Gladys was devastated. Such a hard journey for this! But government representatives arranged for a train to take her and the children to a nearby city where there was an orphanage.

With the children finally safe, Gladys collapsed and was taken to a hospital. She was still suffering from the injuries from her beating, on top of typhus (a disease with fever and a skin rash), pneumonia (a lung disease), malnutrition, and exhaustion.

After she recovered, Gladys went on to open and run other orphanages until she died in Taiwan in 1970.

DISCUSS

It's been said that developing faith is somewhat like learning to dive. If you wait until you're not afraid, you'll never learn. You have to be willing to take the risk before you know how you'll do. What are some risks you could take to develop more spiritual courage?

15

WILLIAM BOOTH

SUPPOSE A BROTHER OR SISTER IS WITHOUT
CLOTHES AND DAILY FOOD. IF ONE OF YOU SAYS TO
HIM, "GO, I WISH YOU WELL; KEEP WARM AND WELL
FED," BUT DOES NOTHING ABOUT HIS PHYSICAL
NEEDS, WHAT GOOD IS IT? (JAMES 2:15–16)

Times were hard in nineteenth-century England. A great number of factories were being built to produce goods, and news of factory jobs drew thousands of poor families to the cities. But the new life there proved to be a nightmare for many of them.

Factory workers were paid poorly, and they worked long hours under terrible conditions. Yet they were forced to pay high taxes. They lived in overcrowded slums in back-to-back houses with no clean water or proper disposal of wastes. Diseases such as cholera spread quickly. Many people tried to forget their troubles in saloons, spending what little they had on alcohol and leaving their families even worse off.

William Booth's father was a builder who also suffered in the hard economic times. When William was thirteen, his father told him that the family had no more money and William would have to quit school. He arranged for William to work for a pawnbroker and learn the trade.

William worked twelve to sixteen hours a day for little money. Often he was so tired at night that he slept in his clothes. On top of that, he hated the pawnbroking business. Every day, poor, desperate people came and left their few treasures in return for a loan with interest. His heart went out to them. He wished he could do something to help.

For a while he thought politics was the answer. He joined a group of people who wanted to get the government to make things better. But he soon gave up on that and started looking for hope elsewhere. He began attending a Wesleyan Methodist church. At fifteen, he trusted in Christ.

William was eager to share his newfound hope. But when he brought a group of ragged boys from the slums to his church, angry church leaders took away his church membership.

After being out of work for a year, he moved to London, where he supported himself by pawnbroking. In his free time he preached on street corners. A Christian businessman was so impressed with what he was doing that he offered to pay William so that he could preach full-time.

That same businessman invited William to a party where he met Catherine, the woman with whom he would share his life and mission. She was a devoted Christian and well educated. Because of health problems, she had spent a great deal of time reading. By the time she was twelve, she had read through the entire Bible four times.

William briefly attended a school for pastors, became a minister, and married Catherine. He didn't stay settled for long, though. He couldn't forget the half-million people in the slums of London, who lived in filth and poverty. His heart broke when he saw half-clothed children fighting over scraps of food or homeless men sleeping in drunken heaps in doorways.

Even though he had a frail wife and four small children, William left his church and salary and became a traveling evangelist. Since the poor people he preached to had no money to pay him, the Booths struggled to make ends meet.

Catherine believed that the apostle Paul's command for women to be quiet when in church referred to idle chatter and not to preaching the Word. She began preaching herself and proved to be a powerful speaker. Soon William started a mission in the poor East End of London, while Catherine preached in churches and summer resorts in the wealthy West End. In this way, she earned money for the family and made William's ministry possible.

He preached wherever he could—on street corners, in tents, or in rented music halls. At first, mobs of Irish attacked the Protestant intruders coming into their neighborhoods. William realized he had to prove he really cared about these people, so he began feeding those who came to hear him preach.

Also realizing that many poor people wouldn't come to dull services, William did his best to make his services interesting. In fact, he used to say he liked religion the same way he liked tea—HOT! He filled his preaching with colorful stories, and he found musicians to play lively music. His unusual methods won many converts—and also many faultfinders.

William thought no one was ever too far gone to save. His motto was Go for Souls and Go for the Worst. Through his ministry, many thieves, gamblers, drunks, and prostitutes became Christians. When their lives were changed, many of them joined him in telling others about the hope they had found.

His work grew. When he saw homeless men lying on a bridge, he rented a warehouse, filled it with beds, and set up a kitchen. By 1872, there were five lunchrooms where the poor could buy a cup of soup for a quarter of a penny or a whole meal for six cents. Thousands of meals were given away free.

In 1878, William and his volunteers became known as the Salvation Army. They wore uniforms and started a band that marched up and down the streets, announcing meetings. The "Army" found more and more ways to help the poor. It provided job training and set up stores that sold food at rock-bottom prices.

Because the people who made matches often came down with a painful, disfiguring condition when phosphorus got in their mouths, William started a factory to manufacture the newly invented, nonpoisonous "safety matches."

The Salvation Army soon spread to other cities. In fact, so many people became Christians and stopped drinking and gambling that the bars and liquor stores lost business. Their angry owners hired hoodlums to attack Salvation Army workers. The worst incident took place in 1882, when a street gang of a thousand people attacked a Salvation Army parade.

By the time he was middle-aged, William was leading a growing Army on five continents. Seven of the Booth children had become preachers and leaders in the Army. Then, in 1890, Catherine died. William was heartbroken but continued to travel and preach. By the time he died in 1912, he had traveled 5 million miles and preached 60,000 sermons.

Today the Salvation Army helps 2.5 million families around the world each year. It has 25,000 officers in 91 countries. The Army's program to help people stop drinking is the largest in the world.

DISCUSS

Think of some non-Christians you know. Are there any practical things you could do for them that might demonstrate God's love to them?

16

A. C. GREEN

WATCH AND PRAY SO THAT YOU WILL NOT FALL INTO
TEMPTATION. THE SPIRIT IS WILLING, BUT THE BODY
IS WEAK. (MATTHEW 26:41)

Except for the grace of God, a childhood accident might have prevented A. C. Green's basketball career from ever happening. Worse yet, it could have ended his life.

A. C. was chasing his cousin. They would run in the front door, through the house, and out the back. His older sister, who was baby-sitting, told them to quit. They didn't listen, so she shut the back door to make them stop. A. C. didn't see the shut door in time, and he ran into it. The glass shattered and slashed his arm from the wrist to the armpit.

At the hospital, his parents were told it wasn't equipped to treat such a serious injury. They rushed to another hospital, where the doctor told them they had gotten there just in time. A. C. would have died if he had lost one more pint of blood. He was taken into surgery immediately. The operation went well. Although his arteries were cut and the gashes were deep, the nerves were still all right.

Except for that accident, A. C. had a happy, normal childhood. His family called him Junior since he was named after his dad. He loved Hamburger Helper, and he dreamed about becoming a professional baseball player.

As a boy, he didn't really stand out in a crowd except for his ability to do wheelies on his bike for a whole block—and for his unusual sense of fashion. He loved colorful striped pants and often wore plaids and stripes at the same time. Long after the styles changed, he was still wearing polyester suits and platform shoes. Sometime during junior high, he learned to dress more acceptably and became one of the "cool" kids.

In high school, most of his friends tried out for basketball, so A. C. did, too. He made the freshmen squad and later the junior varsity.

One day the senior coach saw A. C. play. He put a hand on his shoulder and told him to stick with it because he might have some potential. His words had an impact, for A. C. admired Coach Gray a great deal. The man had coached for thirty years and was well-known for producing winning teams. From then on, A. C. had a goal. With lots of hard work, he made the varsity team where Coach Gray made him do his best.

Until high school, he was an average kid in size, but then he had a growing spurt. As a freshman, he was five feet ten inches tall; when he graduated, he was six feet seven. (By the time he graduated from college, he was six feet nine.)

Coach Gray taught him to be a team player instead of trying to score by himself. Yet A. C. still averaged twenty-seven points per game during his senior year and helped his team win the championship. He was named Player of the Year in Oregon and was on the all-American team. Coaches from big regional universities began recruiting him.

In spite of his athletic success, though, A. C. felt insecure. He was afraid to make decisions. He relied on other people to tell him he was good. In his own words, he was "the biggest people pleaser around."

The summer after his senior year, he took a weekend trip with a group of friends to visit a former teacher who had moved away. The teacher asked the group to go to church with him. When the pastor explained the way to be saved, A. C. realized he needed a personal relationship with Jesus and a bigger purpose in life than playing basketball.

After going forward to accept Christ publicly, he felt free for the first time in his life. All the peer pressure he had felt melted away. He was no longer afraid of other people's opinions.

He headed to Oregon State that fall, a school he chose because it was close to home and known for championship-level basketball. As a brand-new freshman, he was awed by older teammates he'd watched on television, and he wondered if could compete with them. They intimidated him during practice with their roughness and trash talk—telling him he was weak and a loser. But all that made him work harder. His skills steadily improved, and his gift for rebounding became plain.

He also grew spiritually. He became part of a student Bible study group and got up early every day to read his Bible and pray. Although he was nervous about it, he began giving his testimony.

A. C. went on to win the Most Valuable Player award twice. He also attracted attention when he made thirty-nine points in a televised game against Stanford.

After college, he signed up for the NBA draft. When he interviewed, he realized that many NBA teams seemed nervous about his Christianity, but several expressed interest. Secretly he hoped to be chosen by the Lakers, the number-one team at the time. As it happened, the Lakers had the twenty-third pick, and they chose A. C. Now he had to start at the bottom again, playing with basketball greats such as Kareem Abdul-Jabbar and Magic Johnson.

Because he was known as a Christian, he was an oddball in the bunch and had to prove himself on the court. He did. In his second pro game, he scored seventeen points and got sixteen rebounds. He became the first Laker rookie in more than twenty years to appear in every game.

It would have been easy to let his superstar teammates influence his lifestyle, but A. C. learned to admire their talent without copying their character. Professional athletes attract women, and NBA players are known for having relationships with many women. But A. C. had made a promise when he became a Christian not to have sex before he was married. The Laker players teased and tempted him, but he stuck to his standards.

In time they realized his faith was sincere. Several teammates began attending his Bible studies and asked him to tell them about Jesus. During his second season, three teammates made decisions for Christ. Magic often asked him to pray before games. When the Lakers won their second championship in a row, a reporter asked him if this was the greatest moment in his life. He answered, "No, getting saved was."[1]

A. C. played in the NBA finals with the Lakers four times and led his team in rebounds six seasons. After eight years, he moved to the Phoenix Suns, where he stayed several years until he was traded to the Dallas Mavericks. Through it all, he has used his fame to influence young people.

In the late 1980s, he and some friends started the A. C. Green Foundation for Youth. The organization developed Athletes for Abstinence to teach kids that sex outside of marriage is wrong and dangerous. It has also sponsored Special Olympics and sends hundreds of kids to day camps where A. C. teaches basketball and shares his values.

A. C. explains that he tries "to be a river, not a reservoir" so that "money and blessings . . . flow through [him] to others."[2]

D I S C U S S

A. C. resisted temptation. What are some sinful thoughts or actions you frequently struggle with? Have you found anything that helps you avoid or resist their temptation?

17

TIM HANSEL

Even though he has written a best-selling book on Christian joy, choosing to live joyfully doesn't come easily to Tim Hansel. Maintaining a joyful attitude is a daily struggle, because Tim has lived with nausea and pain and never-ending fatigue since 1974.

Tim was an exceptional athlete. He received a football scholarship to Stanford University and started all four years. He also played on a four-time national champion rugby team. He began an exciting teaching and coaching career in 1965. He worked with juvenile delinquents, young people in tough street gangs, and all-American athletes. His teaching took him to the inner city of New York and to seven different countries.

Tim not only challenged his students, but he also pushed himself to achieve high goals. He once ran fifty miles without stopping, climbed one of the highest mountains in the United States, and sailed 25,000 miles in a forty-three-foot boat.

In 1970, he started Summit Expedition, an organization that takes kids and adults on mountain-climbing and wilderness survival trips. Its purpose is to challenge people to do more than they think they can and to get to know themselves and God better.

The turning point in Tim's life came on a mountain-climbing trip to the Sierras. The first day, he and a couple of friends hiked to the Palisade Glacier and set up tents. The second day, they climbed eight hundred feet of snow and ice and then four more lengths of rope. After lunch on top of the mountain (14,000 feet above sea level), they started down.

By late afternoon, though, the snow had changed because of the shade. The bottoms of Tim's boots were now packed with snow, which made their spikes ineffective for gripping. He slipped. He tried to stop himself by swinging his ax into the mountainside. But just as he began to stop, his feet went over the rim of a ledge. Momentum and gravity made him flip upside down before landing on some ice more than fifty feet below.

Once he came to, he was grateful just to be able to move. But he felt wobbly. (He later learned that, because he had landed on the back of his neck, his two-hundred pound body was compressed.) At first he thought he'd had a miracle ending to a very bad fall. However, he still had to make the toughest climb of the day—out of the crevasse and back to their camp.

By the next morning, Tim felt as if he had a migraine headache all over his body. But he hiked more than twenty miles—it took eight hours to reach his car. And then somehow, by

God's grace, he drove himself home. When he got there, he didn't mention the accident—until he woke up during the night in unbelievable pain and didn't know where he was.

At the hospital, Xrays showed fractures in the bones of his spine, crushed discs (the cartilage between vertebrae), and broken pieces of bone in his neck. The doctor told him he wouldn't have been able to climb down the mountain or hike to his car if he hadn't been in shock—and if God had not provided him with extra strength and spiritual resources.

During the next months, Tim's faith was tested as never before. Just walking or getting out of a chair took great effort. He wrote in his journal: "In times like these of such intense physical pain, confusion and doubt, one must simply decide and do, decide and do—and laugh a bit amidst the consequences."[1]

The following spring, Tim was told he'd have to learn to live with never-ending, intense pain the rest of his life. The fall had resulted in a multitude of fractures and crushed discs. It had literally rearranged the muscles in his back. The injuries were beyond repair.

Although the doctors said the damage was permanent, they thought his back was stable enough for him to be as active as the pain would allow him to be. He struggled to keep on climbing, jogging, and playing tennis. Then one day as he delivered a strong serve, he heard a loud crack. He had torn several ribs away from his spine. He spent a week in the hospital and went home in a body cast from his waist up.

The pain became much worse, and Tim went through a time of depression. He realized that he'd have to learn a whole new way of living, because his life was never going to be the way it had been. Using the strongest painkiller available, he tried to keep on working. By the spring of 1976, he was beginning to understand that *all* of life is sacred. Both the happy and the difficult times should be respected as holy and dedicated to God. He discovered he had to "choose either to break *down* or break *through*."[2]

In time, Tim learned new ways to respond to the pain. Through Bible verses such as Nehemiah 8:10, God taught him that though he could not choose to be strong, he could choose to be joyful. When he did that, strength would follow. He realized that happiness is a feeling, but joy is an attitude, a decision, a confident belief that God is in control of every area of life.

In 1976, he wrote his first Christian book, *When I Relax I Feel Guilty*. It was followed by several other bestsellers, including his book about joy in spite of circumstances, *You Gotta Keep Dancin'*.

Tim continued to run Summit Expedition for another fourteen years. But by 1988, his body could no longer meet the demands he was placing upon it. After numerous operations, doctors finally declared him to be "totally and permanently handicapped."

Because of his own problems, Tim and his wife, Anastasia, founded Ignite, Inc., a program that encourages people who live with emotional and physical pain and disability and teaches them to help others in pain. Tim is also a gifted speaker who challenges others to live life to the fullest.

Tim Hansel says that words he wrote more than a decade ago are still true: "Pain is inevitable, but misery is optional."[3] He adds, "No matter what your circumstances, you can still choose to be joyful—and God will give you strength you didn't know was there."[4]

D ISCUSS

What do you think about the following statements? "There is a reason for everything that happens in a Christian's life. God has a purpose for every event that touches a believer." Does this affect the way you respond to pain?

18

JOHN BUNYAN

ALL OVER THE WORLD THIS GOSPEL IS BEARING
FRUIT AND GROWING, JUST AS IT HAS BEEN DOING
AMONG YOU SINCE THE DAY YOU HEARD IT AND
UNDERSTOOD GOD'S GRACE IN ALL ITS TRUTH.

(COLOSSIANS 1:6)

While he was a boy growing up in England during the 1600s, John Bunyan seemed uncon-
cerned with his behavior. He was too busy having a good time playing sports, dancing, and,
later, drinking. He was also known for having a filthy mouth and being a ringleader in all sorts
of mischief.

When he was sixteen, the government made him join the army and fight in the civil war
that was going on. After he came home, he became a tinker like his father. That meant he
traveled to farms and villages to work, repairing pots, kettles, and tools. Because he was poor,
he had to walk from house to house while carrying his heavy anvil (a metal block to hammer
on) and all his tools.

At twenty, John married a pretty girl named Mary. Although most brides brought things
to use in their new homes, Mary too was poor. She only had two religious books. As John
and Mary read the books, though, he realized that many things he did were wrong. So he
tried to change and live the way he thought he should.

John's new "religion" made him miserable. Even though he gave up doing many of the
things he used to enjoy, he still felt bad. He became so depressed that every day seemed filled
with drudgery.

Then one day as he was working in the town of Bedford, he saw a group of poor women
sitting on a doorstep. They were obviously very happy. He got closer and heard them talking
about Jesus. The women were Puritans. They told John that all he had to do to please God
was to ask Jesus to forgive his sins. Once he did that, they said, he would want to serve God
out of love and gratitude, not because he felt he had to earn God's love.

John was very excited. He had never heard about God's mercy and grace before. But at
the time, the law said everyone had to go to the church the government approved—the
Church of England—and that church did not teach the true gospel.

John started going to the women's church. He even moved his family to Bedford to be
close to it. He still had doubts about whether he was saved or not. In fact, he struggled with
doubts about his salvation for years until he read Martin Luther's commentary on Galatians.

Then he finally realized that God *wanted* to have mercy on him.

He was a new man once he was free from his doubts. When the church asked him to preach, his gift for communication became obvious. His vivid imagination painted brilliant pictures with words. Soon people came by the hundreds to hear him preach about the faith he had struggled so hard to find.

Then Mary died, leaving him with four young children. Later, he married a girl named Elizabeth, who turned out to be a brave and loyal wife.

While still supporting his family as a tinker, John traveled long distances to preach to as many people as possible, and he became well-known. He also began to write books about the truths he found in the Bible.

Things became more difficult when England's leader Oliver Cromwell died. He had protected Puritans and Quakers, who worshiped outside the state church. Now, those favoring the king were back in charge. Friends warned John that he would be arrested if he continued to preach. But he kept on, even though he knew he might be hanged. He tried to dodge the king's men by preaching at strange times and in unusual places such as barns and fields.

Nonetheless, he was caught and put in prison. He refused to promise he would quit preaching and was kept in prison for twelve years. It was a terrible time for him. The prison was overcrowded. There was little light and no place to bathe. Typhus, a disease spread by fleas and lice, killed many prisoners. His food was a fourth of a loaf of bread each day. And he deeply missed his wife and children. He worried about them, especially his oldest daughter, who was blind. To help support them, he made and sold thousands of long shoelaces.

At times John was tempted to give in, but he stayed in prison because he wanted to encourage other believers to stand firm through his example. He found strength through reading the Bible and *Foxe's Book of Martyrs*. His prayer life grew deeper, and Jesus became ever more real to him. This led him to write many religious books while he was in jail— including *Pilgrim's Progress,* which described in story form the struggles and fears all Christians face.

John was finally released, but he was free only a few years before he was imprisoned again, this time for six months. By the time he was freed, the government had become more tolerant. He was able to start many churches all around southern England, and he traveled from place to place, helping his little congregations.

Pilgrim's Progress became one of the most popular books ever written. Three hundred years later, it is still in print in more than one hundred languages.

DISCUSS

John Bunyan was able to serve God in a powerful way only after he became completely certain he himself was saved. Do you ever have doubts about your salvation? What do you think it would take to erase those doubts? How can we answer people who struggle with such doubts?

19

CHARLES COLSON

THEREFORE, IF ANYONE IS IN CHRIST, HE IS A NEW
CREATION; THE OLD HAS GONE, THE NEW HAS COME!

(2 CORINTHIANS 5:17)

Chuck Colson had a reputation for being hard-hearted and power hungry. As President Nixon's top legal and political adviser, Chuck was known as the president's "hatchet man." Sometimes he leaked stories to the newspapers to damage a political enemy's reputation. He was a deeply patriotic man, though, and he believed that helping the president was helping the country.

It was a difficult time to be president. American soldiers were dying in Vietnam, fighting a war many citizens didn't think we should be involved in. Even though the war started before President Nixon took office, he was sharply criticized for it. Daniel Ellsberg was one of the men who had helped draw up plans at the beginning of the war. Now he said our country's involvement had been poorly planned.

The president thought that these reports, known as the Pentagon Papers, could put American soldiers in danger and hurt secret talks going on with China. So he ordered Chuck Colson to pass on information to the news media that would make Ellsberg look bad.

Chuck didn't know that two other aides, Howard Hunt and Gordon Liddy, had broken into a doctor's office where Daniel Ellsberg had been a patient. They had also arranged a break-in at the Democratic party's offices in the Watergate building. There they planted spying devices to learn what the Democrats would do in the presidential campaign. Chuck learned about the Watergate break-in on the news.

Several months later, Gordon Liddy and five burglars were charged. The White House tried to cover up its wrongdoing and announced that the burglars had acted on their own. It secretly paid the men "hush money" to keep quiet and pressured the FBI to limit its investigations. But reporters found out and also learned about the break-in at the doctor's office.

Chuck went back to being a private lawyer, while Richard Nixon won a second term in office. A Senate committee investigated the Watergate scandal throughout 1973 and into 1974. Then the president's advisers recommended that he resign. He did, and Gerald Ford became president.

The news media accused Chuck of being behind the Watergate break-in. No one seemed to believe he was innocent. Soon he too was under investigation. Exhausted from all the pressure, he went to visit one of his clients who had become a Christian. The man told

Chuck how Christ had changed his life. He challenged him not to let his pride keep him from finding peace.

Chuck was very moved by this, and within a few weeks he decided to give his life to Jesus. To his dismay, reporters heard he had suddenly become religious, and they made fun of him in cartoons throughout the country. Many people doubted that he had really changed. They assumed that he was faking in order to get sympathy so that he wouldn't be sent to prison.

Once he became a Christian, Chuck Colson wanted to be completely truthful. He pleaded guilty to an offense he hadn't even been charged with—passing out negative information to the press about Daniel Ellsberg.

He went through some very rough times as a new Christian. He worried about the stress his family was under. He was afraid of being put in a prison with men who were there because of laws he had helped pass. Many of his old friends no longer wanted to be seen with him. But a group of Christians stood by him, even men he scarcely knew and men who had been political enemies. They believed in him and encouraged him.

He was eventually sent to a tough prison in Alabama. He had once worn expensive suits and influenced the president. Now he wore a poorly fitting uniform, ran the prison's washing machine, and slept in a room with forty other men, plus some rats and cockroaches. Other prisoners didn't trust him because he had been a government official. He was told it would be safer not to get involved with the prisoners. But he started a prayer group with other prisoners, anyway, because he missed Christian fellowship.

One day a prisoner warned him he had an enemy in the prison who wanted to kill him. Chuck realized that only God could protect him. A short time later, he saw two men walking toward him. He heard a voice inside say, *Now, Chuck,* so he went up and talked to them. One was a former policeman who had been sent to jail for something he had not done. He thought Chuck Colson was responsible. Chuck explained that the investigation had come from the Justice Department, not the White House. He also told the man that he knew what it was like to be a political target. The man shook his hand, and he knew the danger was over.

He often led the other Christians to pray for fellow prisoners, and they saw wonderful answers to their prayers. There were times when he actually praised God for putting him in prison where he could be used.

When he was released, Chuck finished writing a book he'd started in prison. The book described the way Christ had changed his life. He wanted to do more, but he didn't know what. He'd had several promising business offers. He could no longer practice law in Virginia, but he might be able to in Massachusetts. There was also the possibility of doing some kind of prison work, but he wasn't sure he could bear to go back inside a prison.

The answer came to him as he was shaving one morning. He would start an organization to train prisoners so that they could start Christian fellowships in their prisons. In the meantime, his book *Born Again* was published. It became a bestseller and was made into a movie. Now he received invitations to speak at Christian events throughout the country. He used his speaking fees to help pay for his new organization, which he called Prison Fellowship.

He also started speaking in prisons. At times this proved a nerve-racking experience. In

1978, he went into a violent, overcrowded prison in Atlanta. He was warned that there could be trouble. The prisoners were angry. The prison was sweltering.

As he stood in front of eight to nine hundred prisoners, Chuck nervously told them what Christ had done in his own life and what He could do in theirs. He told them Jesus could make them free even while they were in a lousy prison. When he finished, the room erupted in applause. Men stood on their chairs, cheering and clapping. Many men accepted Christ that night, including a former Mafia member known as "Joe the Butcher."

By the end of 1994, 50,000 volunteers were involved in Prison Fellowship. Care Committees have been started to support families of prisoners. Each Christmas, hundreds of thousands of children of prisoners receive presents through the Angel Tree program. Prison Fellowship also offers marriage seminars for inmates and their spouses and support groups for ex-prisoners.

D I S C U S S

In what ways has your life changed because you've accepted Christ? If a non-Christian was watching you, what do you think he would notice was different about you because of your faith?

20
JEAN DRISCOLL

AND WHATEVER YOU DO, WHETHER IN WORD
OR DEED, DO IT ALL IN THE NAME OF THE
LORD JESUS, GIVING THANKS TO GOD
THE FATHER THROUGH HIM. (COLOSSIANS 3:17)

Jean Driscoll was born with spina bifida. That is a defect where part of the spinal cord is exposed. Doctors thought she would never walk. But they didn't know how much energy and determination Jean would have.

Jean was an active toddler. She got around by creeping on her hands and feet, even though she had heavy metal braces on her legs. Her mother remembers that she went through two pairs of shoes a week because she was so quick and determined.

She started to walk when she was two. Years later, her daily cab ride to school never got her there on time, so she asked a friend to teach her to ride a bicycle. She learned to ride without her parents knowing. Jean's mom was shocked when she saw her daughter—braces and all—steering a two-wheeler.

Jean continued to bike until she was fourteen. One day she took a corner too sharply and fell. Her hip hit the pavement and was dislocated. She had five hip operations and spent a year in a complete body cast. She missed a year and a half of high school. She finally got the cast off only to dislocate the hip again just by sitting up in bed. There wasn't enough muscle strength in her lower body to hold her body together.

Jean became angry. The prospect of life in a wheelchair overwhelmed her. She battled thoughts of suicide and feelings of worthlessness. Her parents took her to healing services, but no miracles came. When Christians told her she wasn't healed because she didn't have enough faith, she turned away from God.

Well-meaning friends told her that the only thing she could become was a secretary, since secretaries sit down when they work. But Jean planned to become a nurse, and she headed to the university. However, a painful pressure sore that tunneled down to the bone landed her in the hospital again and kept her from focusing on her studies. Her grades plummeted, and she flunked her freshman year.

A major turning point in Jean's life came when she agreed to become a "mother's helper" for a Christian nurse. That nurse talked her into trying church again. And the more Jean learned about Christ's love, the less bitterness she felt. In 1986, she gave her heart to Jesus.

Not long after that, she transferred to the University of Illinois and started playing on the women's wheelchair basketball team. She was determined to show others how well a disabled person could perform, and she trained hard seven days a week. Her striving for excellence left little time for church or spiritual growth.

Jean's coach was impressed by her determination and hard work and encouraged her to train for the Boston Marathon's wheelchair division. Jean entered the race, hoping to come in third. She surprised herself and everyone else by coming in first and setting a world record.

In 1991, she not only won her second Boston Marathon but also the Women's Sports Foundation's Amateur Sportswoman of the Year Award. Debbie Richardson, a new member of the university's athletic department, was assigned to plan a ceremony to honor Jean's achievement. The two women soon became close friends. Debbie was a committed Christian, and Jean began going to church with her and praying with her.

She recommitted her life to Christ just before the 1992 Olympics. From that time on, she has focused on giving God glory on and off the racetrack. She has grown closer to God through Bible study, prayer, and Christian fellowship and has learned to depend on His strength so that she can do her best as she trains and races. When she won the silver medal in Barcelona, she shared the victory with her church family.

Jean has now won the Boston Marathon six times and a gold medal in the Paralympics. She has had countless opportunities to give God credit for her victories in newspaper and magazine articles, speaking engagements, television appearances, and her involvement with Fellowship of Christian Athletes.

Discuss

What are some of the most important goals in your life right now? What are your motives behind those goals? What enables a Christian to have purer motives?

21
DAVE ROEVER

FOR YOU CREATED MY INMOST BEING; YOU KNIT
ME TOGETHER IN MY MOTHER'S WOMB. I PRAISE
YOU BECAUSE I AM FEARFULLY AND WONDERFULLY
MADE; YOUR WORKS ARE WONDERFUL, I KNOW
THAT FULL WELL. (PSALM 139:13–14)

Dave Roever was born in Brownsville, Texas, but his family didn't stay there long. His father was a pastor who started new churches, and he moved on once the churches got on their feet. His mother, who was ill much of Dave's life, grew close to God through her pain.

Dave accepted Christ when he was five years old. Later, he dreamed of becoming an evangelist. He also loved music and became an excellent jazz guitarist. In his teens he played in a band until the songs and the places the group played didn't feel right to him.

During high school, Dave began preaching at youth camps. He also fell in love with a strong Christian girl named Brenda. While attending a Bible college in Texas, Dave married Brenda and then was drafted into the navy to serve in the Vietnam War. Because he was studying to be a pastor, Dave probably could have gotten excused from his obligation. But he didn't try. Even though he hated to leave his new bride, he felt it was his duty to serve his country.

Dave did so well in the navy's basic training that he was chosen to train for river patrol— one of the most dangerous assignments in Vietnam. His patrol and prisoner of war training included severe hardship and harsh treatment, but Dave graduated with the highest scores in the class.

Even that didn't prepare him for the nightmare he soon faced. It was his group's job to go out looking for Communist soldiers (who looked like everyone else in Vietnam). The patrol moved up and down the river, in constant danger of being fired on by enemy soldiers hiding in the jungle. Each firefight left Dave thrilled to be alive but sickened from seeing all those who died.

To make matters harder, other soldiers made fun of him because he didn't drink and because he stayed faithful to his wife. And then his commander learned that Dave had studied to preach. He bought Dave an electric guitar and a microphone and made him the unofficial pastor of the base. Many soldiers realized that he really believed what he talked about.

A tragedy proved that to the rest. One day on patrol, Dave got ready to throw a special grenade designed to burn jungle brush and to reveal hidden booby traps. But the grenade was defective, and it blew up in his hand.

Dave's body caught on fire. He dropped into the river, but he continued to burn. In unimaginable pain he crawled out of the water, calling out, "God, I still believe in You." He was barely conscious as he was put into a helicopter. Third-degree burns covered 40 percent of his body. At one point the medics thought he was dead.

They rushed him to the nearest hospital, but he wasn't expected to live. By some miracle he did. Later, when he saw himself in a mirror, he wished he hadn't. Not only was he in excruciating pain, but half of his face was gone. He felt like a monster.

Once Dave's condition was stable, he was brought back to a hospital in the United States. Now his wife would be allowed to see him. He was anxious about Brenda's reaction. What if she shrank back in horror when she saw him? But he worried needlessly. When Brenda came into his room, she kissed him tenderly and said, "Welcome home, Davey. I love you."

Dave was in the hospital fourteen months, undergoing painful treatment for his burns. When he was released, he faced more pain—from other people's reactions. Small children cried with fear when they saw him.

The first time he tried to preach in a church, the congregation looked shocked and horrified. A wave of depression and doubt washed over him. How could he fulfill his dream of becoming an evangelist? He felt like a freak from a circus sideshow. But when several men came forward to accept Christ after he spoke, he began to feel hopeful.

Since then, Dave Roever has undergone many surgeries to improve his appearance. Every morning he untapes his eyelid (which won't close on its own), puts on his hairpiece, and attaches his plastic ear. Even so, the damage the fire inflicted is still obvious. Children still stare. Adults peek, while pretending not to be looking.

Dave has struggled with feeling inferior and unacceptable. But he also has found a deep sense of worth in God's unlimited, never-ending love. That love has given him the confidence to travel throughout the States and other countries, holding crusades and telling others about God's love and peace. He has appeared on Billy Graham crusades and done a weekly television program. Because he's wrestled with his own inferiority feelings, he is especially effective in reaching out to teenagers who don't like themselves and believe that no one else does, either.

DISCUSS

Do you ever feel bad about your appearance, abilities, or personality? Do you sometimes wish you were different? What are some truths that can help Christians accept themselves as they are?

22
WILLIAM TYNDALE

"GIVE TO CAESAR WHAT IS CAESAR'S,
AND TO GOD WHAT IS GOD'S." (MATTHEW 22:21)

England's king and his helpers sent spies to Europe to track him down, but William Tyndale avoided capture for ten years. What awful crime had this quiet man done to be at the top of England's Most Wanted list? Even his enemies admitted that his life was a model of holiness. His only crime was translating the Bible into English.

In the 1500s, England had only one church (Roman Catholic), which had a great deal of wealth and power. The government allowed the church to enforce its rules on everyone. The church required people to pay large amounts of money but did little to help them. Many were so poor that they lived in slums. Yet the pope's representative to England, Cardinal Wolsey, lived in a palace with five hundred servants.

All of the Bibles in England were written in Latin. Translating any part of the Bible without permission from the church was against the law. The church leaders thought putting the Bible into the language of the common people would somehow cheapen it. They were also afraid that people would question some of the church's teachings once they could read the Bible themselves.

Anyone who read the Scriptures in English could lose his land, his belongings, and his life. Those who did so were considered enemies of the church and the government. Men and women who dared teach their children the Lord's Prayer or the Ten Commandments in English were burned to death.

William had a brilliant mind. He had gone to Oxford University while still a young lad, and he eagerly studied languages and logic before becoming a priest. He had mastered seven languages. His study of the Scriptures had put a burning fire in his soul to change things that were wrong. It angered him that many of the priests who taught the people didn't know themselves what the Bible said because they couldn't read Latin.

After he finished his studies at Oxford and later Cambridge, he became a tutor to a wealthy family and preached in a village church. William taught that we are saved not by what we do but by faith in Jesus Christ. When his sermons angered the local leaders, he moved to London. Then he tried to get the bishop to give him approval to translate and print the Bible in English. The bishop refused. But a wealthy businessman who liked William's preaching agreed to help. He advised William to move to Germany and work on his translation there. William could then send him the printed copies, and he would smuggle them into England in bags of grain.

William worked tirelessly as he translated the New Testament from Greek. He was a gifted man, who chose each word carefully. Although he kept the language simple so that any Englishman could understand it, it had beauty and rhythm much like poetry. Once William's New Testament made its way to England, the demand was so great that other printers made more and more copies.

The church leaders were outraged. They fought back by arresting, imprisoning, and killing anyone caught with William's Bibles. Warned that there was a warrant for his arrest, William moved frequently as he worked on the Old Testament. One time a drunken printer talked about him in front of one of the spies sent to find him. William was warned in the nick of time and barely escaped with his precious translation.

He also wrote books explaining the teachings of Christianity, including one King Henry VIII liked. Called *Obedience of a Christian Man,* it encouraged people to obey the government unless it required them to do something against God's laws. About the same time, King Henry was quarreling with the pope, who didn't want to grant the king a divorce. As their dispute grew, the king became more powerful and the church became weaker.

After his divorce, the king became more friendly toward Englishmen who had been exiled because of their beliefs. So William relaxed a little. About this time he met a young man named Henry Phillips, who pretended to want to learn about spiritual things. William befriended him, but Phillips led him into a trap, and he was arrested.

For four months William was thrown into a cold dungeon near Brussels in Belgium and was not allowed any visitors. His good attitude impressed his jailer so much that the jailer became a Christian. But William was finally condemned as a heretic—an enemy of God—and was sentenced to be strangled and then burned in 1536. His final words as he was tied to the stake were "Lord, open the king of England's eyes."

William Tyndale's prayer was answered. Shortly after his death, a friend printed a Bible (including all of William's translation) and dedicated it to Henry VIII. It was the first English Bible allowed to circulate without persecution. Later, William's translation provided more than 90 percent of the wording of the King James Bible, authorized by the king in 1611. It became the most influential book in history. It is still used today.

DISCUSS

Explain how William Tyndale's life illustrated Matthew 22:21. Why is it especially important for Christians to be obedient to the government? Can you think of times a government might require Christians to do something against their beliefs? What can we do to prevent things like that from happening in America?

23
KAY COLE JAMES

AM I NOW TRYING TO WIN THE APPROVAL OF MEN,
OR OF GOD? OR AM I TRYING TO PLEASE MEN? IF I
WERE STILL TRYING TO PLEASE MEN, I WOULD NOT
BE A SERVANT OF CHRIST. (GALATIANS 1:10)

Her father and brothers weren't home the hot June night Kay Cole was born. They were hunting bullfrogs in the swamp so that her mother could fry them for supper. There wasn't a doctor around, either. The only black doctor in Portsmouth, Virginia, couldn't be located. So a neighbor and a nurse-midwife helped in the birth.

Kay was the only daughter in a poor black family with six children. Her father had a brilliant mind and loved classical music. He had been a champion debater in high school and had won several singing contests. He had dreamed of becoming a chemist or a doctor, but he couldn't afford to go to college. Frustrated because he was stuck in lowly jobs, he began to drink heavily.

Kay's mother came from a well-respected family in Richmond. All of her mother's sisters went to college and became professional people. They were middle-class blacks at a time when that was a very rare thing. Since Kay's father was unable to hold a job because of his drinking, her mother's family persuaded them to move to Richmond.

The town of Richmond was completely segregated. That meant blacks couldn't ride at the front of the buses. They couldn't use public libraries or swim in public pools. Kay never even had a conversation with a white person until she reached junior high school.

After Kay's father began hitting his wife and older sons, her mom left him and moved the family into a public housing project. Their five-room apartment had a cement floor, walls made of cement blocks, and hundreds of cockroaches. Kay sang in bed to take her mind off the cockroaches that came out when the lights went off.

Some people thought they were lazy or low class because the government paid their rent. They called her family "project niggers." Kay worked hard to get good grades, achieve success, and live right to prove her worth to the people who looked down on her.

Kay's mother got on a bus in the early morning, went to her sisters' homes to cook and clean for them, and came home after sunset. Only four-feet-seven-inches tall, she had a strong, homegrown faith in Jesus. She took her kids to church on Sundays and wouldn't allow any swearing. When her sons stole chickens because they wanted fried chicken so badly, she threw the birds out. They'd starve, she said, before she'd allow stolen food in their home.

One day Mrs. Cole tearfully said she was sending Kay to live with a wealthy aunt and uncle who didn't have any children. She knew they could give her the things she couldn't—including a college education.

Kay desperately missed her mother and brothers. To make things worse, her aunt also was an alcoholic. When she drank, she criticized Kay cruelly. At times she would crumple up her homework, scream that it was all wrong (even when the answers were right), and call her stupid and ignorant. Once again, Kay was being sent the message that she was worthless, inferior, and dumb.

Life became still more difficult when the Supreme Court outlawed segregation in public schools. Kay was one of twenty-six black students sent to a junior high with three hundred whites. Many of the white students resented the blacks and made their lives miserable.

Kay was pricked with pins while walking to class. Sometimes she was stuck so many times that she had to hold her dress against her body to keep blood from dripping down her legs. She was pushed down the stairs. Teachers gave her papers D's and F's to prove that black children couldn't compete with whites. But the black students hired tutors and worked even harder. After a while, teachers began to grade fairly, and Kay's grades rose to A's and B's.

In church she heard that she was God's beloved child, created in His image. This gave her a sense of worth and dignity that her aunt and hateful whites couldn't destroy. The church also taught her that hate destroys the spirit but love builds it up.

She began reading her Bible every night. She became less concerned with proving herself to others and more concerned with pleasing God. In college she became involved in Inter-Varsity Christian Fellowship. Through Bible studies and prayer meetings she realized that God had not only created her but He had created her black. She found a new pride in being black. For the first time, she got to know many white people who were kind and loving.

Following Jesus was not a popular thing to do among the many black students who considered Christianity a religion for whites. At times they ridiculed and harassed her. She didn't enjoy the friction, but Kay would later realize that God was preparing her for what she would face in the future.

She graduated and was hired as a manager with AT&T. Because of affirmative action laws, businesses in the early seventies were looking for educated blacks to hire so they would have their minimum percentage of minority employees.

Kay married Charles James and began to move up in the phone company. She quit work when they had children, but she began volunteering at a crisis pregnancy center and became committed to preventing abortions. After they moved to another city, she went to work for a chain of stores and helped to start a crisis pregnancy center there.

With a growing family and a busy job, Kay felt she was too busy when she was asked to speak for the pro-life position on a black cable TV show. But her husband reminded her of how strongly they both felt about abortion, and she agreed. Then she learned the program would be aired live nationally during prime time, and she was scared to death. She didn't sleep the night before and kept thinking how awful it would be if she threw up on national television.

She faced a woman who had argued the proabortion side many times and was well armed with statistics and polls to make it sound right. Kay felt ill-prepared. All she had was a strong belief that abortion was wrong. But that proved to be enough. She did so well in the debate that the National Right to Life Committee asked her to become their national spokesperson.

The next three years were a whirlwind of traveling, debating, giving speeches, and holding press conferences. Too busy doing to spend much time learning, Kay often felt poorly prepared and very nervous. For weeks before big debates, she couldn't sleep or eat properly. At times she knew the audience would be hostile, and fear clouded her thinking. She learned to cry out to God for help. "Every debate was really a stretching out in faith," she recalls, "and I learned to trust God for wisdom and even for the very words I would speak."[1]

Although mail poured in saying her message had touched people, Kay resigned after three years. She wanted to spend more time with her family and to take care of her mother who was dying of cancer.

DISCUSS

Describe a time when you (1) didn't stand up for something you knew was right, because you were outnumbered or (2) did take a courageous stand in spite of what others said or thought.

24

DENNIS BYRD

THESE [TRIALS] HAVE COME SO THAT YOUR FAITH—
OF GREATER WORTH THAN GOLD, WHICH PERISHES
EVEN THOUGH REFINED BY FIRE—MAY BE PROVED
GENUINE AND MAY RESULT IN PRAISE, GLORY AND
HONOR WHEN JESUS CHRIST IS REVEALED. (1 PETER 1:7)

Growing up in Oklahoma, Dennis Byrd and his two older brothers played their own brand of rough football. They also performed in a family puppet ministry in different churches. The Byrds were committed Christians who went to church Sunday morning and Sunday and Wednesday nights. The other evenings, Dennis's father read the Bible to the family and explained it.

The family was rich in faith and love but short on money. When Dennis was nine, they moved to California and lived with his father's father. Dennis was a freshman in high school when they moved back to Oklahoma. There they lived in a small town with his mother's mother. The boys stayed in an RV camper while his parents and sisters lived with his grandmother in her trailer. Like his brothers before him, he started playing high school football.

During his junior year, the family moved again—to the countryside. Dennis's dad had made a deal with a partner to develop a new subdivision and build homes in exchange for ten acres of land. Because all of their money was tied up in getting the development going, the Byrd family lived in a trailer and an old school bus. Unfortunately, the development deal fell apart, and they lost nearly everything they had.

Dennis knew the only way he'd be able to go to college was on a football scholarship. To build his strength, he came up with a unique training program. He sank a four-by-four green oak post into the ground. Then he practiced slamming the wood with his hands or forearms until sweat poured off his body and his hands bled. He also spent hours working out in the school's weight room.

He wound up setting a state record in high school football with thirty-nine sacks. College coaches started coming around to recruit him. He decided to go to college in Tulsa, where he married a girl named Angela.

After college, Dennis was drafted to play for the New York Jets. They gave him a three-year contract for $1.2 million with a fourth-year option and a $250,000 signing bonus. He was called a "hybrid" player—a blend of quickness, speed, and size. With all of his success, though, he never forgot his faith. He had a habit of praying before games and drawing a fish on his socks to let people know he was a Christian. He and Angela belonged to a Bible study group and traveled to different states telling young people about their faith.

In the summer of 1992, Dennis felt a strange anxiety that something that would test his faith was about to happen. He decided to take out an insurance policy that would pay if he was injured. Many injuries led to a bad season for the Jets, and he prayed for an opportunity to be a witness to his teammates.

The opportunity soon came in an unexpected way in a game against the Kansas City Chiefs. As the Chiefs quarterback took the snap and dropped back to pass, Dennis flew around their offensive line. His focus was on the quarterback he wanted to sack. But just before he dove to make the tackle, the quarterback stepped forward. This caused Dennis to miss him and collide with his own teammate. And he didn't see the player coming at him soon enough to position his head correctly to absorb the hit.

When he came to, he was lying on the ground, unable to move his legs or control his arms. Doctors soon discovered his fifth cervical vertebra, at the base of his neck, was fractured.

Throughout the following painful and frightening days, weeks, and months, Dennis and Angela prayed for God's strength—and received it. Screws were put in both sides of his head and then attached to a steel band circling his skull to keep his head and neck from moving. He was also put into a tight, shell-like, plastic vest, somewhat similar to the chest armor Roman soldiers wore. The pressure from the heavy vest made breathing an effort.

Doctors operated for seven hours, trying to repair the bone and putting in three steel plates to stabilize his neck. They also prescribed an experimental drug but told Dennis it might be years before they'd know if he would walk again.

There were many lonely, uncertain nights and weeks of torturous physical therapy. Before the accident, he had been able to bench-press 430 pounds and squat-lift 800. In the weeks following the accident, he had to ask nurses and attendants to do everything for him. He also had to be turned every two hours to keep ulcers from forming on his skin. Later, he struggled just to push a skateboard a couple of inches and worked for hours learning to do simple tasks such as brushing his teeth and combing his hair.

Through it all, he spent much time reading Bible verses and praying. He specifically prayed for strength to accept whatever the outcome would be and to become a witness through the situation.

Dennis was elated the first time he was able to wiggle his toe. Two months after the accident, he took his first steps. At press conferences and interviews, he gave the glory to Jesus. In a live interview during the Rose Bowl, he told the announcer, "Without question, the biggest factor in my life has been my faith in Jesus Christ. That's been able to keep me going whenever the times are really tough. It's been a hard two months, but God's given us the strength every day."[1]

Dennis eventually wrote a book about his ordeal and developed an organization to help send disabled kids to a special summer camp.

D I S C U S S

It's been said the most powerful witness comes when the stones are flying. What do you think this means? (If you need help, see Acts 7:59–60.) Have you ever been touched by someone's faith during a very difficult time?

25

HEATHER WHITESTONE McCALLUM

INSTEAD, [YOUR BEAUTY] SHOULD BE THAT OF YOUR
INNER SELF, THE UNFADING BEAUTY OF A GENTLE
AND QUIET SPIRIT, WHICH IS OF GREAT WORTH IN
GOD'S SIGHT. (1 PETER 3:4)

In 1974, a tiny toddler named Heather Whitestone lay in a hospital bed in Dothan, Alabama, fighting for her life. Heather was a bright, active child before coming down with a fever that wouldn't go away. Instead, it rose higher and higher as her hands, feet, and joints swelled. Heather had a rare but deadly virus.

In desperation, her doctors finally gave her injections of two extremely powerful antibiotics—and she began to improve. At the end of two weeks, she was released from the hospital. She was then given months of physical therapy and special vitamin supplements. She regained her health, but she had lost something she'd never get back—95 percent of her hearing.

Heather was almost totally deaf. Specialists said she would probably never develop much speech or achieve more than a third-grade education. Her mother, Daphne, learned sign language, talked to experts, and read books on deaf education. She discovered there was a chance Heather could learn to talk *if* she learned very young. If they waited until she was four or five, it could be too late.

To do so, she would have to learn to use what little hearing she had. In those days, no hearing aid that fit in the ear was powerful enough to help her. She had to wear a hearing aid strapped on her chest with cords that ran up to each ear. She hated it, but it did help her to hear a little bit.

Her mother realized that Heather would not try to learn to speak if they continued to use sign language with her. But once they stopped that, communicating became difficult and frustrating for Heather. It took her six years to learn to say her last name correctly. She took speech therapy and had what seemed endless homework with her mother repeating words to her over and over. (Most young children need to hear a word twenty or thirty times to use it in conversation, but a hearing-impaired child may need to have a word repeated hundreds and hundreds of times.)

Heather began to take dance lessons when she was five. Her mother thought dance would help her feel vibrations and hear high and low pitches. That would help her listen to speech. Dance did that for her. It also became one of the great loves of Heather's life.

It was fortunate that she had something she enjoyed so deeply, because school was a struggle for many years. She was tested at the end of her kindergarten year. Part of the test showed she was intellectually gifted. The verbal part showed she had a vocabulary of only around 250 words. The average six-year-old uses about 2,500 words. From then on, Heather's teachers used a small microphone that broadcast to a receiver she wore. This made her hearing aid more helpful.

Desperately wanting to be like her big sisters and everyone else, Heather pushed herself harder. She often worked on speech therapy and schoolwork until ten at night and then got up early to work some more. But she always made time for dance lessons and practice.

Although she was good at math and memorized facts easily, she continued to lag far behind her classmates in reading. It was frustrating to work so hard and still be at the bottom. She often felt lonely and unaccepted. One day in fourth grade, she came home crying and told her mother, "Other kids not like me. Not be friends. Because Heather different."[1]

Then she read a book about a deaf girl who went to a special school. She decided she wanted to do that, too. Her mother said no at first. She was afraid Heather would lose all the progress they had worked so hard for. But as time went by, Heather grew more frustrated and unhappy. By the time she was eleven, her parents agreed to send her to a school for the deaf in Missouri. After three years, Heather had made enough progress to return home.

She had been very popular among other deaf students, but in public high school she again felt left out. She wore her hair so that it covered her hearing aid, and she tried to fit in. But she realized that many teenagers wanted to be around only "perfect people." Still, she was happy to be home so they could all "be a family" again. Things weren't that simple, however, for her parents divorced.

Heather attended church and Sunday school, although she missed much of what was taught because of her deafness. Televised church services became important to her because the camera closeups allowed her to read lips. The TV programs and Bible reading touched her life. When she was a junior in high school, she trusted Christ as her personal Savior.

Heather graduated from high school with honors and began college. She knew her mom couldn't afford to pay all of her expenses, and she started looking for ways to help out. Then a friend suggested she use her dancing talent and enter a beauty pageant to earn the scholarship money. She won $1,400 and was encouraged to enter other contests.

After winning several local competitions, Heather entered the Miss Alabama contest and became first runner-up. By this time she knew that Miss America had a great opportunity to reach other people's lives and help them. She wanted that opportunity. She entered the Miss Alabama pageant the next year and was again chosen first runner-up. On her third try, she was crowned Miss Alabama and went on to compete in the Miss America pageant.

She won the talent competition with a moving ballet interpretation of Christ's crucifixion, danced to the Christian song "Via Dolorosa." The audience and judges were amazed that someone nearly totally deaf could dance so beautifully. Heather explained that she first listened to the music with an amplifier, then counted with the music and memorized it.

Heather didn't react when her name was announced as Miss America for 1995—she didn't hear the announcement! It was only when another contestant pointed to her and said,

"You won!" that she understood. At twenty-one years of age, Heather Whitestone had become the first person with a disability ever to become Miss America.

During her year's reign, Heather tried to be a bridge between hearing and nonhearing people. She tried to encourage others with disabilities. She did her best to be a good role model, telling young people that she didn't smoke, take drugs, drink, or have sex because she wanted to please the Lord. She also explained her faith and told how God helped her accept her deafness.

Because of the difficulties she's experienced, Heather is a kind and caring person who has learned to find her strength and peace in the Lord. No doubt her inner beauty is one of the reasons she was one of the most popular Miss Americas in pageant history.

D I S C U S S

List some of the people who care most about you. How much do you think your appearance matters to them? How much does their appearance matter to you? How important is your appearance to God? Do you spend more time and effort developing your character or polishing your image?

26

JAMES DOBSON

FINALLY, BE STRONG IN THE LORD AND IN HIS
MIGHTY POWER. PUT ON THE FULL ARMOR OF GOD
SO THAT YOU CAN TAKE YOUR STAND AGAINST THE
DEVIL'S SCHEMES. (EPHESIANS 6:10–11)

The 1960s were a stormy time in America's history. There was widespread drug use. There was violence between blacks and whites. There was anger over the Vietnam War. Young people turned against the government, their parents, religion, and rules in general. Alarmed at the direction the country was headed, Dr. James Dobson set out to do something about it.

He was the son of a tenderhearted evangelist and great man of prayer. James himself was a strong Christian who worked at a children's hospital in California and taught at the University of Southern California's medical school.

In his spare time James began counseling, speaking, and writing. He believed the Bible had the answers to life's problems, and he urged people to turn back to the values many were turning away from. The first book he wrote, *Dare to Discipline,* called for better discipline in the schools and taught parents how to be the leaders in their homes. It quickly became a bestseller.

Soon James was being asked to speak in many places throughout the country. He became so busy that he had little time left for his wife, Shirley, and their two children. Something had to change.

Though he loved teaching at the medical school, he wanted to help as many people as possible. In the end, he decided to give up his secure position with the university and start his own organization, which he called Focus on the Family.

With a grant from Tyndale House Publishers, James rented a two-room office, hired a part-time secretary, and began a radio program heard once a week on forty-three stations.

Even though James and Shirley daily asked the Lord to bless their efforts, they weren't prepared for the amazing response they received. After a few months, they were flooded with mail, phone calls, speaking invitations, and requests for counseling. James hired and trained more staff to help with the mail and phone calls.

Unfortunately, in those early days, few of the people who asked for help remembered to support Focus on the Family financially. By the fall of 1979 the ministry owed $30,000 more than it had. James and his family asked God to show them what He wanted them to do.

Within thirty days, Focus on the Family received more than $60,000, and Word Publishers brought out a series of films shot during one of James's seminars. Over time, those films would be seen by 70 million people around the world. They caused Focus to grow at an unbelievable rate.

In the beginning, James's goal was to do whatever he could to help Christian families become stronger. As time went on, though, he realized that many non-Christians were also searching for ways to make their homes healthier and happier. He wanted to do more than give them practical advice; he wanted to introduce as many as he could to the Lord. To do this, Focus began broadcasting stories of people whose lives had been dramatically changed by Christ.

He didn't stop there. He has worked tirelessly and courageously to stop groups with ideas that would tear down morals and hurt families. He believes America is in the middle of a "civil war" over values, and he is determined to do everything within his power to fight for what's right.

Several presidents have asked him what government can do to make homes stronger. Other political leaders have fought what he has tried to do. News reporters who don't agree with his ideals have harshly criticized him. He has even been sued for his work against pornography (pictures showing immoral sex).

James helped start the Family Research Council, which works to get laws passed to help American families. He has spoken out against abortion. He has worked to protect religious freedom and has urged young people to stay sexually pure.

Focus on the Family broadcasts are now heard by 650 million people in ninety-five different countries. In addition to its broadcasts, the organization now carries on more than seventy other ministries. These include producing Christian books, magazines, and videos for adults and children, providing counseling, and holding basketball camps where inner-city children are introduced to Christ.

DISCUSS

When James Dobson began writing and speaking about God's plan for families, he had no idea where it would lead. But few men in recent times have done as much to change our country for the better. What are some ways we could make a difference?

27

RUTH BELL GRAHAM

BUT MAY THE RIGHTEOUS BE GLAD AND REJOICE
BEFORE GOD; MAY THEY BE HAPPY AND JOYFUL.

(PSALM 68:3)

While living in China with her missionary parents, Ruth Bell often heard gunshots from warlords and bandits roaming the countryside. When Japan invaded China, it was common to hear air-raid bells and see Japanese bombers flying over her home. But even with all of China's problems, Ruth had a deep love for the country and its people. And mostly she remembers her childhood as a happy time. In fact, she was brokenhearted when she had to leave China at the age of thirteen to go to boarding school in Korea. She was terribly homesick and lonely and often cried herself to sleep until she learned to depend on God to help and comfort her. As she looked back years later, though, she believed God used this time to prepare her for a lifetime of good-byes.

Once she accepted having to be away from home, Ruth enjoyed her school years. Her bent for mischief came out as she rubbed shoe polish on the backs of doorknobs and put clay snakes in shadowy corners. Yet China was never out of her thoughts and prayers.

By the time she went on to Wheaton College in Illinois, she was a beautiful young woman and had many dates. She was determined, however, to remain single. She didn't want anything to keep her from becoming a missionary to China—until she met a student named Billy Graham.

At first, Ruth tried to talk Billy into going to China, too. But as she prayed and got to know him better, she realized that God had called him to preach. She was torn between her own dream, her love for Billy, and her feeling that God had a special purpose for him. Eventually, she decided to help Billy follow God's plan for his life.

They married, and she concentrated on making a happy home even though the demands of his work often made that difficult.

He was the pastor of a small church for a year and then became a traveling evangelist. This meant he and Ruth were separated for weeks and sometimes for months at a time. Later, with Billy rarely at home, she was left alone to train and discipline their five children. She handled nearly all of the problems, usually not mentioning them to him so that he wouldn't worry while he was away. She also made ends meet during the early years when Billy's income was very low.

When tourists started coming to their home night and day, it became obvious that the

Grahams needed to find a place with more privacy. They bought some land in the mountains. Ruth planned a charming log house, found leftover lumber, supervised the mountain men who built it, and even did some of the carpentry herself.

Because of Billy's fame, she often felt the rest of the world was watching them, expecting the whole family to be perfect. She could have become angry or harsh when her sons became rebellious during their teens. Instead, she just kept on praying and loving them until they both came back to Christ.

Sometimes she missed Billy so badly that she took one of his old sport coats to bed with her. But she hid her tears from the children, and she always kept good-byes brief to keep her emotions under control. As soon as he was gone, she would tell the children, "Let's look forward to his coming back. We have to learn to make the least of all that goes and the most of all that comes."[1] Often she launched into a big project such as spring cleaning or refinishing furniture to keep her mind off her loneliness.

Through all the sacrifices and pressures, Ruth Graham was (and is) a joy to be near. She has a delightful sense of humor and a playful spirit. In her fifties, she took up hang gliding. After she was a grandmother, she borrowed her son's leather jacket and took off on a Harley Davidson motorcycle, winding up in a ditch once and a lake another time. Later, she fell out of a tree while putting up a swing for her grandchildren.

Not only did she make their home a place of love and joy, but she also supported Billy's ministry in numberless ways. She loves to read and usually keeps four books with her at a time. Many of the examples in Billy's sermons are from books she has shared with him. He once commented, "She seems to know something about everything. Some of my best thoughts come from her."[2] Ruth has also done research for some of his books and regularly offers wise advice and encouragement.

Throughout her life she has managed to keep a thankful spirit and find happiness in every situation by keeping her eyes on Jesus. From the beginning, she made time with Him a priority. When her children were young, she got up at 5:00 in the morning to study the Bible and pray before they woke up.

Over the years, Ruth Graham has worn out several Bibles and memorized hundreds of verses. She has confided in Christ, and He has encouraged her. The joy of the Lord has been her strength. Now in her late seventies and in constant pain from severe arthritis, Ruth rarely complains but carries on cheerfully as always.

DISCUSS

Do you think most people who know you would consider you a cheerful person? Are you cheerful when things aren't necessarily going your way? What are some things we can do to get rid of a bad mood?

28
WETHERELL JOHNSON

SHOULD YOU THEN SEEK GREAT THINGS FOR
YOURSELF? SEEK THEM NOT. (JEREMIAH 45:5)

Wetherell Johnson grew up in a Christian home in England. She believed in God, but she didn't give her life to Him when she was young. Still, she found comfort in her beliefs—until her parents sent her to France to be educated. There she spent time with people who put down the Bible, and Wetherell lost what faith she did have.

She knew her skeptical attitude toward Christianity would hurt her godly parents, so she kept her doubts to herself. Her life became empty, and she felt depressed. As she looked for something to give life meaning, a Bible verse she had once learned kept coming back to her: "Whoever lives and believes in me will never die. Do you believe this?" (John 11:26).

One day as Wetherell thought about that verse, God showed her that Jesus was truly His Son. With tears of joy she finally gave her life to Him. Because one verse made such a difference in her life, Bible study became very important to her. She took five Bible courses through the mail and began teaching a class of rough girls.

In time, she knew God wanted her to become a missionary. She trained as a nurse and in mission work and went to China in 1936. In those days most Chinese worshiped evil spirits and relatives who had died. The hot, humid climate took a toll on Wetherell's health. After an appendix operation, she was not expected to live.

Japan was at war with China and was bombing the country. At the same time, Communist rebels were fighting to control the government. Wetherell had to move frequently because of the dangers. Once, six Japanese soldiers came to her home and threatened her, putting their knifelike bayonets to her neck. Often she felt overwhelmed by problems and loneliness. But time after time she found the strength and comfort she needed in God's Word.

One day an order came that every missionary would be put in Japanese prison camps with other "enemy aliens." Wetherell was taken to a camp with two thousand other foreigners and shut in an old horse stable. The building wasn't insulated. In the summer it was stifling hot. In the winter there was no heating, even when the temperature was fifteen degrees below zero. It was one hundred feet by fifty feet and housed eighty-nine people. Beds had only two to three feet between them. Because they were so crowded, people got on each other's nerves and often argued.

The prisoners were given a small amount of rice for breakfast and lunch. In the evening they got rice and a one-inch cube of meat. In the beginning, Wetherell carefully picked the worms out of her rice, but she soon realized she needed the protein and ate them too. At night she and the other prisoners strapped tight belts around their waists so that their hunger pains wouldn't be so bad. During three years in the camp, she lost thirty-nine pounds.

Then World War Two ended, and she returned to England to regain her health. After a couple of years, she was back in China—even though fighting between the Communists and the government was worse than ever. As the Communists took over more and more land, it became very dangerous for missionaries to stay. They bravely worked on, though, trying to train as many Chinese Christian leaders as they could before the country fell to Communist rule.

Finally, afraid she would cause problems for the Chinese Christians if she stayed any longer, Wetherell left China. She went to the United States to visit friends and began speaking in churches and at conferences.

At one church, five ladies came up to her after she'd spoken and asked her to lead them in a Bible study. She hesitated at first. These women already knew quite a bit about the Bible, and there were many churches they could attend to hear God's Word. She longed to teach people who had never heard about Jesus—such as the millions of Chinese.

But as she prayed about the women's request, God reminded her of Jeremiah 45:5. She felt God was asking her, "Cannot you do this small thing for me?"[1] So she agreed, but she insisted the ladies work at learning. She assigned Scripture passages for them to study before class and gave them questions to answer. During each class time, she talked about the verses, and the women discussed what they had learned. At the end of each meeting, she gave them notes to take home and review.

Their group, called Bible Study Fellowship, grew quickly. Soon Wetherell divided the class into smaller groups and trained other leaders. When people heard about Bible Study Fellowship, she was asked to start groups in other cities.

Eventually there were BSF groups all over the United States, and Wetherell wrote a five-year study course. Within six years, 100,000 women were involved. Later, men's Bible studies were begun, and BSF spread to Australia, England, Canada, and New Zealand.

Thousands who have come to BSF classes to learn more about the Bible have ended up giving their lives to the Lord.

DISCUSS

Sometimes we think a small act of kindness or some encouraging words won't really make a difference, but God can use our small efforts. Think of three or four little ways you could show God's love to someone this week.

29
SAMUEL LAMB

THE LORD IS MY HELPER; I WILL NOT BE AFRAID.
WHAT CAN MAN DO TO ME? (HEBREWS 13:6)

Samuel Lamb was born in China in 1924. His parents were Christians who modeled trust in God and obedience. He was a small, frail child who often had infections in his lungs. At five, he became so ill from diphtheria that a doctor said he had no chance of living. But he did live, and it is said his mother told him, "God touched you because He needs you." Later, during World War Two, a Japanese bomb barely missed him. Again Samuel felt that God had spared his life for a special reason.

During his teens and early twenties, he developed many abilities that would one day help him serve God. He went to a boarding school in Hong Kong, where he learned to speak English. In college he became a gifted concert pianist, learned to give his classmates haircuts, memorized large portions of Scripture, and went beyond his required studies to become a pastor.

After the war, the new Chinese government tried to stop all religious groups except the official church (a church that claimed the Bible was not accurate and that Christ was not really God). The government restrictions caused Christians to start worshiping in homes. Samuel began a church in his home with thirty members.

He was speaking at a church in a nearby city one day when he met a lovely Christian woman named Sing Yin. Believing she was God's choice for him, he asked her to marry him the following year. Samuel and Sing Yin deeply loved the Lord, one another, and the two children who later blessed their home.

By 1955, the government said that not cooperating with the official church and its beliefs was the same as not obeying the government. Samuel knew that if he continued to preach the complete Word of God he would be in danger. But he obeyed God, anyway. Soon the government declared that house churches with more than thirty-five people were illegal, and Samuel was arrested.

He was not allowed to attend his own trial. Witnesses who defended him were soon silenced. People who had never been to his church lied about what he preached. In prison he risked further punishment and death by witnessing to the other prisoners. He also wrote several hymns, even though he was not allowed to sing. After a year and a half, he was set free because of the lack of evidence against him.

Without hesitating, he went back to leading his house church. It soon grew to more than one hundred members. Less than a year later, he was again arrested. This time he was sentenced to twenty years of hard labor.

First, Samuel was sent to a livestock and tea plantation. Although he barely weighed a hundred pounds, he was forced to work at removing old tea shrubs with a shovel, pick, and ax. After they had worked long hours in the fields, prisoners were given some cabbage soup and for several more hours were forced to listen to talks on being better Communists. Sometimes the pain and exhaustion seemed too much to bear, but he found comfort by remembering Bible verses such as "I can do all things through Christ who strengthens me."

As he worked and as he lay on his insect-covered bed, Samuel strained to remember more Bible verses. Many prisoners noticed his kindness and spiritual strength and quietly asked him about his faith. Risking severe punishment, he led them to the Lord. Eventually, he was assigned to office work and was later made the camp barber. Because he cut the prisoners' hair one at a time, he was able to do more witnessing and to encourage other Christians.

After five years, he met a prisoner who had a New Testament. The man let him use it. Samuel made handwritten copies of as much Scripture as he could late at night—until a guard caught him. The guard took away the Bible and Samuel's copies.

For punishment, he was moved to a coal mine, where the work was even harder than the fieldwork had been. The mines were dark, dirty, and dangerous. Coal dust got in his lungs and weakened his body. All day long he strained his muscles almost beyond endurance and then was forced to sit through eight- to twelve-hour lectures on Communism. Others lost hope, but Samuel felt the Lord was always with him.

Finally he was released, and he rushed home to Sing Yin—only to learn that she was dead. Communist soldiers had taken most of the family's belongings, part of their home, and all of Samuel's Bibles and books. His sister had been able to find another Bible somewhere, which he gratefully read for hours at a time.

Once more, he began holding church services in his home. This time the congregation grew to thirteen hundred members, who came on different days of the week. Police and other officials threatened him several times.

And then China started opening its doors to the Western world. People representing President Reagan, and later President Bush, visited Samuel. Billy Graham featured him on one of his television programs. News reporters from different countries broadcast reports of the trouble the Chinese government gave him. This attention helped protect Samuel and his church from further punishment. But police still tried to frighten him and sometimes seized his teaching materials.

By 1980 he was the best-known house church pastor in China. Other pastors traveled hundreds of miles to learn from him. Churches listened to cassettes of his teaching and passed them on to other churches. Thousands of copies of the booklets he wrote were spread throughout China.

DISCUSS

As Christians in America, we are not put in jail or threatened by police because of what we believe. Still, what are some ways that fear of people can keep us from living for Christ?

30

ABRAHAM LINCOLN

On reaching Jerusalem, Jesus entered the temple area and began driving out those who were buying and selling there. He overturned the tables of the money changers and the benches of those selling doves. (Mark 11:15)

When Abe Lincoln was a young man, a wealthy farmer hired him to take vegetables and fruit down the Mississippi River. After all the produce had been sold or traded, Abe went sightseeing in New Orleans.

What he saw changed his life. He was horrified to see black men, women, and children being sold the same way horses and cattle were sold. Buyers felt the slaves' muscles. They looked at their teeth. They watched to see how fast they could run. He saw frightened slaves cry when they were taken away from their families.

From that moment on, Abe hated slavery. He told friends if he ever got a chance, he would hit it and hit it hard. At the time, it didn't seem likely he would ever have any power to stop slavery. His family was poor, and he was a grade-school dropout. But he worked hard, and he read every book he could get his hands on. He studied law books and became a lawyer.

He became widely known for his honesty and fairness. Friends encouraged him to run for office in the government. At first, he lost more elections than he won. But finally he was elected to represent Illinois in the United States House of Representatives. Later, he ran for the United States Senate and lost.

In his second race for the Senate, he ran against a famous senator named Stephen Douglas. The debates the two men had on slavery were widely reported. Abe lost again, but so many people were impressed by his sincerity that he became the Republican party's candidate for president in the next election. He went on to win, even though his name wasn't even on the ballot in ten Southern states.

Three months passed from the time Abe was elected until he actually became president. In the meantime, many Southern states voted to leave the country and start their own nation, the Confederacy. This was not legal under the Constitution, and the Northern states wouldn't let them go without a fight.

It was a time of great hatred as the country split over the slavery question. Abe spent many sleepless nights and lost forty pounds from the heavy stress. Every mail delivery brought death threats and warnings. Close friends begged him to resign before taking the oath of office. When a plan to kill him on the way to Washington was discovered, he traveled in disguise and under heavy guard.

As president, Abe did everything in his power to prevent the Civil War. He even came up with a plan to pay Southern slave owners for the slaves they'd lose, if they'd lay down their guns. In spite of his efforts, fighting between North and South broke out soon after he took office.

It was a long and bitter war, and hundreds of thousands were killed. The deaths on both sides broke the president's tender heart. Many times he broke down and wept openly. He spent his nights praying and grieving for his country. He spent his days meeting with people with special needs because of the war.

Abe Lincoln was a deeply religious man. During the darkest hour of the war, he called for a national day of prayer, which we observe to this day. Although he did his best to follow the Bible's teachings, during most of his life he felt tremendous guilt for not being good enough. That changed when his son Willie died. Willie's nurse told the president about her personal relationship with Christ and encouraged him to know Jesus the same way. He later told a friend that he had given himself to Christ and found the peace he had always longed for.

Even though he hated slavery, Abe never hated those who practiced it. When he took the oath of office for his second term as president, he asked the country to put aside bitterness. He called on both sides to care for each other and to work together for a fair and lasting peace. When the North won the final battles, he told his leaders not to punish Southern soldiers but instead allow them to go back to their homes as quickly as possible.

The weary president granted many, many pardons and made plans to rebuild the Southern states and bring them back into the Union. But one evening he took a much needed break to attend a play with his wife, and the evening had a tragic end. As he watched the play, he was shot and killed by an actor who was mentally ill.

More than ten thousand books have been written about the man many consider to be our greatest president.

DISCUSS

Why do you think the verse from Mark goes with this story? What are some things in our society that should make Christians angry? What can we learn from Abraham Lincoln's example of dealing with wrongdoers?

31

MILLARD FULLER

Millard Fuller owned a direct mail and publishing business in Alabama. It was so successful that he had become a millionaire. But his workaholic habits had ruined his marriage.

In 1965, his wife, Linda, moved to New York. Millard went to a Christian community in Georgia named Koinonia Farm to sort things out. He realized that their lives had gotten off track and that they both needed to come back to the Lord. He went to New York and began repairing his marriage.

As Millard and Linda prayed about God's plan for their lives, they became convinced that He wanted them to sell their business and give away the money to the poor. After they did that, they worked in Christian ministries for a couple of years and then moved to Koinonia Farm. While there, Millard and other Christians came up with a plan to build houses and sell them to needy families with interest-free loans. This made the houses much more affordable, since most home buyers pay for their homes two times with normal interest rates.

The group raised money through donations and loans. As owners paid for their homes, money came back in to build more houses. By 1972, twenty-seven homes had been built and more were on the way.

The next year Millard and Linda left on a special missionary assignment in Africa. During the three years they were there, they started a housing project in Zaire and helped eighty families move into new homes. Since so many Africans were in desperate need, the Fullers wanted to build many more, but they didn't know where the money would come from.

They went back to Georgia and started Habitat for Humanity. This organization raises money, recruits volunteers, and furnishes plans and know-how so that God's people throughout the world can have decent housing. Millard bought an old house for $4,000 that doubled as Habitat's first headquarters and his law office.

Knowing how badly the poor need a sense of pride and dignity, he decided not to give away any homes. Habitat provides a hand up instead of a handout by making homes affordable to the poor but not free. All labor is done by volunteers, and homes are sold without profit. Part of the materials is often donated. The homeowners invest three hundred to five hundred hours of their own labor into their house and other Habitat houses.

In the United States alone, 20 million people live in very poor housing or are homeless. An example of the kind of people Habitat has helped is an Appalachian family of eight who lived in a twelve-by-twelve-foot log house with no plumbing or electricity. The father worked in a canvas factory, but he made only $125 a week.

Habitat built that family a well-insulated, four-bedroom, 820-square-foot house. To keep the home affordable, plumbing was not included, but room was left for it to be added later. The payments were only twenty-five dollars a month for eighteen years. The family was thrilled to finally have a warm home that didn't leak.

Because one-fourth of the world's population lacks decent housing, Habitat has a goal to build at least one house overseas every time they build a house in the United States. Homes in third-world (poor) countries are often smaller and made out of different materials so that they can be affordable even where incomes are very low. In some cases, houses have tin roofs and walls of cement or clay bricks and cost as little as $600. While humble, these durable homes are much better than the cornstalk-and-mud huts they often replace.

But Habitat does more than build good homes for people who've never had them. Along the way it builds friendships and shows the love of Jesus. All kinds of people work together on each house—rich, poor, teenagers, senior citizens, and people from many different kinds of churches. In some cases, prisoners who have been allowed to work alongside Christian volunteers have come to know the Lord themselves.

Dedication services are held every time a home is finished. The homeowner is given a Bible, and everyone present gives thanks and praise to the Lord. New owners are often so overcome with joy that they are unable to speak. Many turn around and volunteer to work on other houses so that someone else can be blessed as they have been.

Now that Millard and Linda's children are grown, they travel around the world, taking part in building, raising financial support, and sharing the Habitat vision. In 1996, Millard received the Presidential Medal of Freedom. In 1997, a Habitat house was completed somewhere in the world about every fifty minutes. He hopes to have completed 100,000 homes by the year 2000.[1]

DISCUSS

Millard Fuller believes everyone could have a simple, decent place to live if enough people cared enough to make it happen. The problem, he says, is that even Christians are often more interested in getting more for themselves than in giving to others. What do you think?

32

DWIGHT L. MOODY

I CAME TO YOU IN WEAKNESS AND FEAR, AND
WITH MUCH TREMBLING. MY MESSAGE AND MY
PREACHING WERE NOT WITH WISE AND PERSUASIVE
WORDS, BUT WITH A DEMONSTRATION OF THE
SPIRIT'S POWER, SO THAT YOUR FAITH MIGHT NOT
REST ON MEN'S WISDOM, BUT ON GOD'S POWER.

(1 CORINTHIANS 2:3–5)

While growing up, Dwight L. Moody seemed a highly unlikely choice to become the greatest traveling preacher of the nineteenth century. He was a poor, uneducated farm boy. His father died when he was four, and Dwight quit school after the fifth grade.

He wasn't interested in farming. He left his home in his teens and headed to Boston where he sold shoes in his uncle's store. Although he came from a Christian home, Dwight wasn't interested in religion, either. He attended church but only because his uncle made him go.

One day Dwight's Sunday school teacher came to the shoe store. The man told him that Christ loved him and wanted his love in return. He urged Dwight to give his heart to Christ. He did, and his life was never the same.

Dwight Moody was so excited about his faith that he couldn't keep it to himself. As he studied the Bible and grew spiritually, he started telling what he had learned at his church's weekly prayer meetings. Unfortunately, some of the educated people there didn't like his poor grammar, folksy stories, and loud way of talking. Realizing that he didn't "fit in" in Boston, he moved to Chicago.

There he became so successful selling shoes that he set a goal to make $100,000. That was a fortune in the 1850s. In the meantime, he used his free time to go to the poorest part of town and invite children to his Sunday school class at a nearby mission. Like a happy uncle, he gave them rides on his pony and handed out candy and inexpensive gifts. His love drew boys and girls like a magnet, and his Sunday school grew from twelve students to fifteen hundred. Along the way he added more and more teachers and found bigger and bigger buildings to hold classes.

His life goal changed when one of his Sunday school teachers told him he was moving away because he was dying. Before the man left, he wanted Dwight to go with him to visit each of the girls from his class to ask them to accept Jesus. Every girl they called on that night asked Christ into her life. After that, Dwight no longer cared about selling shoes or making money. He wanted to spend all of his time being a missionary to Chicago.

He served the Lord with energy and enthusiasm. He told people on the streets about God. He led prayer meetings for the newly organized YMCA. He raised money to build the world's first YMCA building. The Sunday school he started grew into a church that later became known as Moody Memorial Church. During the Civil War, he was a chaplain to the soldiers. He also married a lovely Christian woman named Emma Revell.

When Emma became ill, a doctor suggested that he take her to England. While they were there, he went to a prayer meeting where a speaker said, "The world has yet to see what God can do with one man wholly committed to Him."

Dwight L. Moody decided to follow God completely and see what God would do with him. After returning to Chicago, he became well-known and started speaking in cities throughout the States.

In 1871, he was asked to hold meetings in England. His first night speaking at Cambridge University was a dreadful failure. The highly educated students disrupted the service by making fun of him and laughing loudly. The next night, he began by telling them they had behaved in a very ungentlemanly way the night before and that they could show their apology by listening politely this time. He won their interest and their respect. By the time he finished, some of the students who had earlier made fun of him gave their lives to Christ. He went on to hold many successful meetings in England and Scotland.

Even without radio and television to broadcast his messages, he became known in other countries. His sermons were reprinted in newspapers and books. During his forty years of ministry, he was often criticized for his simple way of talking and for his poor grammar. Yet more than 100 million people heard or read the gospel because of D. L. Moody.

In spite of his own limited educational background, he started three schools. He started girls' and boys' schools in his hometown to give a Christian education to those who couldn't afford one. He also began a college in Chicago to train Christian workers. That school, known today as Moody Bible Institute, has sent more than six thousand missionaries to other countries.

All this came about because D. L. Moody wanted to see what God could do "with one man wholly committed to Him."

DISCUSS

Have there been times you didn't tell someone about Jesus because you didn't think you knew the Bible well enough or because you might not do a good job? In what way might that show a lack of faith?

33

JOSH McDOWELL

I DESIRE TO DO YOUR WILL, O MY GOD; YOUR LAW IS
WITHIN MY HEART. (PSALM 40:8)

Young Josh McDowell's motto was Where There's a Will, There's a Way. He developed determination early in life because he had so much to overcome.

Josh was naturally left-handed, but when he went to school his teachers made him use his right hand. One teacher snapped at him and smacked the table whenever he used his left. Josh became so frustrated that he started stuttering. While practicing speeches at home, he could speak perfectly, but in front of the class his stomach twisted into knots and he started to stutter. Then his teacher scolded him for that.

He had even bigger problems. He grew up hating his father. His dad was an alcoholic who lost several jobs because of his drinking and who often beat Josh's mother. When Josh got older, he sometimes tied up his dad in the barn to keep him from hurting his mom. During his last year of high school, his mother tearfully told him she couldn't take the abuse anymore. She only wanted to live long enough to see him graduate. She died four months later.

Since he got no financial help from his father, Josh had to work to pay his own way when he went to college in Michigan. In spite of hard work, he got off to a rocky start. His English teacher told him his grades were poor because his grammar and pronunciation were bad. He talked the way most of the country people talked where he grew up. But that wasn't acceptable among city people. His teacher believed in him, however, and helped him with his grammar. She suggested he record himself and listen for his mistakes.

He worked harder than ever and taught himself to improve his memory as well. His grades went from straight D's to straight A's, and he was voted class president. He planned to become a lawyer and then go into politics. He even wrote out a detailed, twenty-five-year plan that ended with his becoming governor of his state.

Because he was very outgoing, Josh knew most of the other students. He noticed that one group seemed different from everyone else, and he wondered why. When he found out they were Christians, he told them he didn't believe in religion. They dared him to look at the reasons Christianity made sense.

One of his class assignments was to work on one big term paper for a whole year. He decided he would write a paper proving that Christianity couldn't be true, based on historical facts. But the more he read, the more he became convinced the Bible told the truth. One night he asked Jesus to come into his life and forgive his sins.

Josh's life began to change. The hatred he'd felt for his father melted away; he began to love him. He told his dad why his feelings had changed, and his father became a Christian, too. He never drank again.

Josh moved on to a Christian college in Illinois. He started speaking to Sunday school classes and youth groups. He still planned to become a lawyer and speak in churches in his spare time. Later he realized that God wanted him to go into Christian work.

It wasn't easy to give up all of his ambitions, but after he graduated from college he went to seminary, a school for pastors. He also started working for Campus Crusade, witnessing to students at a nearby college.

When he'd finished his training, Josh went to work for Campus Crusade full-time. However, they already had a speaker, so he never got to speak to large groups—something he loved to do. It was four years before he was finally asked to teach at the Crusade's Bible school. He was very excited about this, and he worked for six months to get ready.

At the last minute, he was asked instead to see that everything ran smoothly at a huge staff training. He was disappointed to be working behind the scenes again. Things got worse when many of the seventeen hundred people who had come to the conference became ill with diarrhea. Because the meetings were in an old building, the overworked restrooms broke down. He put in twenty-hour days plunging toilets and mopping up.

Exhausted and now sick himself, Josh became resentful. After all, he hadn't gone to seminary to clean restrooms. Then he remembered how Jesus had washed His disciples' feet, and his whole attitude changed. He was ready to do whatever he could to serve others.

God honored his obedience. During the late 1960s, he was sent to witness on college campuses in South America. Most of the students he talked to hated Americans. Some of them became so angry when he tried to teach about Christ that they threatened to kill him. But Josh convinced many that Jesus really was God's Son.

Since then, he has spoken to young people all over America. His books, TV specials, films, cassettes, and appearances have reached millions. God has also blessed Josh with a wonderful family—all because he changed his motto to Where There's a Will, There's a Way, if It's *God's* Will."

DISCUSS

What are your dreams for your life? Would you be willing to give them up if you believed God wanted you to do something else?

34

ELIZABETH FRY

DO NOT JUDGE, OR YOU TOO WILL BE JUDGED. FOR
IN THE SAME WAY YOU JUDGE OTHERS, YOU WILL BE
JUDGED, AND WITH THE MEASURE YOU USE, IT WILL
BE MEASURED TO YOU. (MATTHEW 7:1–2)

The Gurney family considered themselves Quakers (a group of Christians known for their simple lifestyle). But their religion didn't keep them from enjoying the finest parties England had to offer in the late 1700s. Like her widowed father and sisters, Elizabeth Gurney enjoyed a colorful, shallow life until she was seventeen. At that time she heard a visiting preacher talk about the true meaning of being a Quaker, and Elizabeth's life was never the same.

Much to her family's dismay, she abandoned her fancy clothes, gave up music and dancing, and became a serious Quaker. She began gathering poor children together every Sunday evening and teaching them Bible stories. When she saw where and how the children lived, she wanted to do more for them and their families.

She married Joseph Fry, a wealthy Quaker, and she began to help the poor in practical ways. Even though she soon had children of her own, she found time to go out into the slums of London.

Gathering up her long skirts, she would make her way through narrow passages and up broken stairways. She brought clothes and medicine for any who needed them, and she brought her Bible to teach everyone about the Lord.

One day Elizabeth heard another Quaker speak about the terrible conditions women lived under at Newgate Prison. She could easily have told herself that she was too busy to get involved. By this time she had eight children. (She eventually had eleven.) But she went to the prison to pray with the women prisoners.

At first, the jailors wouldn't let her go inside. They told her they themselves never went inside alone. It was too dangerous. The women were a wild mob, they warned, who would tear off her clothes and take her things. But Elizabeth would not be discouraged. She had a letter from the governor of the prison granting her permission to go in, and she insisted on going in alone.

No doubt she had second thoughts once inside. She was soon surrounded by three hundred screaming women who behaved like beasts, fighting, clawing, and swearing. Some had children. Many were nearly naked. All were dirty. They were crowded together in four small, foul-smelling rooms. There were no beds—only three levels of hammocks. The prison didn't provide clothing or bedding or give the women anything to do. They were, however, allowed to buy alcohol with coins they got from begging through the bars.

If Elizabeth had shown any fear, she would have been in serious trouble. But she kept her gaze steady as she picked up a dirty child and told the women they must all do something for the children. She told them she would start a school if they would help.

Most women of her day and especially of her social background would have looked at the prisoners with total disgust and considered them worthless. But Elizabeth treated them with respect. One of the first Scripture passages she taught from was Isaiah 53:6, which says *everyone* has sinned and Christ came to take *everyone's* sins away.

After seeing how great the needs were, Elizabeth convinced other Quakers to join her. They provided clothing for the prisoners and started a school for the children. They also brought materials to teach the women to knit and sew so that they would be able to earn money. To take part, the women had to promise to give up drinking, bad language, and other wrong behavior.

Elizabeth taught them about the Bible. She reached out to the women individually in friendship—telling of her faith, praying with them, and comforting those who were to be executed or sent overseas to convict colonies.

Her trust and respect woke something in the prisoners. She gave them a sense of dignity. They were human beings created in God's image and loved by Him, regardless of what they had done. In time, officials were amazed at the change in them.

In 1818, Elizabeth was asked to talk about her prison work before the House of Commons (England's lawmakers). After that, letters and requests for help poured in. She had made the world aware of the evils in prisons and showed, through her own kindness, that things could be different. Soon she was traveling around Europe, urging governments to treat prisoners better and teaching them how. Whenever the job seemed overwhelming, she would say, "I feel the rock always underneath me."[1]

Still, Elizabeth couldn't close her eyes to others who were suffering. Six hours after hearing that a man had frozen to death on the streets of London, she had a committee working to set up a shelter for the homeless. Later on, that committee also provided warm bedding and food and found jobs for the unemployed.

She organized classes for poor children, started more than five hundred libraries for coast guardsmen throughout Britain, and founded a school to train nurses.

On her deathbed, Elizabeth could say, "Since my heart was touched at seventeen . . . I never have awakened from sleep, in sickness or in health, by day or night, without my first waking thought being how best I might serve my Lord."[2]

DISCUSS

It's been said that Elizabeth Fry loved the unlovable into loveliness. Have you ever considered someone a hopeless case, not worth your time or interest? How can we maintain a loving attitude toward such people?

35

HUDSON TAYLOR

COMMIT YOUR WAY TO THE LORD; TRUST IN HIM
AND HE WILL DO THIS: HE WILL MAKE YOUR RIGH-
TEOUSNESS SHINE LIKE THE DAWN, THE JUSTICE OF
YOUR CAUSE LIKE THE NOONDAY SUN. (PSALM 37:5–6)

From the beginning, Hudson Taylor's life was greatly influenced by prayer. Before he was born, in 1832, his parents prayed he would become a missionary to China. At the exact time his mother prayed for his salvation, he accepted Christ. He was deeply touched by his father's frequent prayers for the vast country of China, where few had ever heard about Jesus.

As soon as Hudson decided to go to China, he did his best to prepare himself. Because he was frail and sickly, he began exercising and building up his health. In addition to studying Chinese, Greek, Hebrew, and Latin, he worked as an assistant to a busy doctor to learn more about medicine.

He also found a way to strengthen his faith. The doctor he worked for was absentminded and often forgot to pay him on time. Instead of reminding the doctor, Hudson prayed and trusted God to take care of his needs. Several times he had little or no money left when his food ran out and his rent was due, but God always supplied what he needed.

It was during such a time that a poor man asked him to come and pray for his wife, who was desperately ill. The man told him he didn't have any money for medicine or to feed his family. The sight of the man's starving children broke Hudson's heart. He didn't know what to do. All he had was one small coin, and he was out of food himself.

He struggled for a few minutes, then gave the coin to the grateful man and went on his way. The next day someone sent Hudson a pair of nice gloves. Inside one of them was a coin worth four times as much as the one he had given the man.

In China, Hudson's faith was tested again and again. He was alone among thousands of people who looked at him with curiosity, dislike, and suspicion. He witnessed and preached for many months with no results. The new missionary society that had promised to send him money seldom sent anything.

He found strength and answers in trusting God and in prayer. Later, he shared the lesson he'd learned with friends: "Depend upon it. God's work, done in God's way, will never lack God's supplies."[1]

Hudson realized that his English clothing and looks distracted the Chinese. He bought Chinese robes, dyed his hair black, and attached a pigtail. The Chinese felt complimented, and they respected him in return.

Then he went deeper into the country, where few foreigners had ever gone. He also fell in love with an English girl who worked in a mission school and married her.

After six years of working in China, he became ill and went back to England with his wife and child. But during the next five years, he couldn't stop thinking of the million Chinese people who died each month without knowing God. He translated the Bible into Chinese, completed his medical training, and prayed for more missionaries.

When he couldn't persuade any missionary societies in England to send people to China, he decided that he would have to start his own mission. But he didn't know how he could ask others to take the risks that would be involved. He became so upset about it that he nearly had a nervous breakdown. But finally he realized that the welfare of the new missionaries would not be his responsibility but God's. Then he peacefully prayed for twenty-four more missionaries to China.

Within a year his prayer was answered. The China Inland Mission was started, and Hudson and his family went back to China with the new volunteers. Again he faced hard times. His oldest child died. Some of the new missionaries didn't agree with his methods and caused problems. His beloved wife died at the age of thirty-three after giving birth to their sixth child. The baby also died. The mission's money often ran out.

Through it all, Hudson's faith grew, and God answered his prayers. He wrote a friend, "We have twenty-seven cents and all the promises of God." Soon afterward, a letter came with $4,000 to broaden the ministry.[2]

He went back to England again and spoke of all the lost souls in China while he prayed for seventy more missionaries. He never asked for money, but money poured in, and seventy new workers left for China. The next year he asked God for one hundred, and one hundred two sailed.

The greatest trial of all was the Boxer Rebellion of 1900. Chinese who hated foreigners killed many missionaries and Chinese Christians and destroyed their property. Hudson was in England when he heard about all of his missionaries who had been killed. It was almost more than he could bear. "I cannot read," he wrote. "I cannot pray, I can scarcely even think—but I can trust."[3]

God greatly honored Hudson Taylor's faith. By the time he died at the age of seventy-two, there were 849 missionaries in China and 125,000 Chinese Christians.

DISCUSS

Why do you think some Christians have so much more faith than others? What steps can we take to help our own faith grow stronger?

36
GEORGE WASHINGTON CARVER

BUT JOSEPH SAID TO THEM, . . . "YOU INTENDED TO
HARM ME, BUT GOD INTENDED IT FOR GOOD TO
ACCOMPLISH WHAT IS NOW BEING DONE, THE SAVING
OF MANY LIVES. SO THEN, DON'T BE AFRAID. I WILL
PROVIDE FOR YOU AND YOUR CHILDREN."

(GENESIS 50:19–21)

George Washington Carver was born in Missouri near the end of the Civil War. Both of his parents were slaves. Shortly after he was born, his father died, and George and his mother were kidnapped by the Ku Klux Klan. Their owners, Moses and Susan Carver, really cared for them and were heartbroken. They hired a man to find them and buy them back, but the man found only George.

George was sick when he was returned. Mrs. Carver nursed him back to life, but he was weak most of his childhood. His future didn't look bright, either. He was a black orphan, growing up during a time when thousands of former slaves were struggling to find ways to earn a living. The South had been crushed by the Civil War, wealthy people had become poor, and many blamed the blacks for their problems. Because he was a Christian, George trusted God to help him through the difficulties he faced.

George was very intelligent. He loved to learn, but he had only one book, and there were no schools in his town that allowed black children to attend. When he was ten, he asked the Carvers if he could go to a town that had a school for blacks. The Carvers agreed, but they couldn't afford to give him any money. He did odd jobs for other people until he had saved a dollar. Then he set off, not knowing where he would sleep or how he would eat.

Once he got to the town, he slept in a haymow until a Christian black couple took him in. He studied hard and did laundry work and other odd jobs to help pay his way at school. Within two years, he had learned everything his untrained teacher could teach him. He moved to Kansas, because he'd heard *everyone* could go to school for free there.

Now George was totally on his own. He supported himself by washing clothes, cooking, and working as a handyman while he went to school. Finally, he graduated from high school. His friends thought he'd be satisfied with that. Very few black people went to college back then. But he was determined to get more education so that he'd be able to help other black people.

He mailed an application to a college and was thrilled when a letter came saying he was accepted. But when George showed up, they wouldn't let him stay after they saw that he was black.

With broken dreams and no money, he turned to farming for several years. Then he heard about a college in Iowa that took black students. Even though he was now twenty-six years old, he sold his farm, bought some laundry equipment, and headed for Iowa. He arrived at the college with ten cents. He used that to buy cornmeal and cooking fat, which he ate for a week until his laundry business got started.

At first George studied art. His paintings were beautiful, and his teachers told him he could become a great artist. But, although he loved art, he decided God wanted him to teach other blacks better ways to grow food. So he switched to another college that had agriculture courses.

He eventually earned a master's degree. Because of his unusual abilities, he was asked to teach at the college and was put in charge of the school's greenhouses and experiment station. Soon he was a well-respected plant scientist, making a large salary.

One day another black man—Booker T. Washington—asked him to come and teach at his new trade school for blacks in Alabama. Feeling this was God's plan, George left his good job and went to the poor Tuskegee Institute. He was given a very small salary, few supplies, no textbooks, and no laboratory equipment. He and his first students made equipment out of things they found in the trash. After a time, his hard work and brilliant mind helped make Tuskegee a well-known school.

George also did more than anyone else to make the South successful again. Southern farmers were having a hard time getting crops to grow. He knew this was because cotton had been grown there for hundreds of years, and cotton wore out the soil. He told farmers that they should plant something that would build the soil up again—such as sweet potatoes or peanuts.

However, few people wanted to buy peanuts at that time. George prayed about the problem. Then he did many experiments until he found three hundred products that could be made from peanuts and more than one hundred uses for sweet potatoes.

During World War One, he helped the Army by showing them how to dry food so that it wouldn't spoil when it was shipped overseas. When wheat flour became scarce, he taught the Army cooks to bake with his sweet potato flour.

George Washington Carver was happy to help everyone who asked, whether they were white or black. He never charged for his advice, and he saved most of his salary to help poor students get an education.

DISCUSS

It's been said that hardship makes people either bitter or better. In what ways did George Carver become better because of the difficulties he faced? Have you ever gone through a hardship? Did it change you? How?

37
DAVID LIVINGSTONE

EVEN NOW THE REAPER DRAWS HIS WAGES, EVEN
NOW HE HARVESTS THE CROP FOR ETERNAL LIFE, SO
THAT THE SOWER AND THE REAPER MAY BE GLAD
TOGETHER. THUS THE SAYING "ONE SOWS AND
ANOTHER REAPS" IS TRUE. (JOHN 4:36–37)

The best-known missionary of all time led only one man to Christ, and that man eventually turned his back on Christianity. Yet more than a hundred books have been written about this missionary, because he planted seeds of the gospel, plowed paths for others to follow, and changed the course of a whole continent.

A harsh childhood in Scotland helped prepare David Livingstone for the extreme hardships he would later face. He was born in 1813 during his country's industrial revolution (a time when the way goods were made changed from handmade to factory-made). His family was poor; all seven of them lived in a ten-by-fourteen-foot room.

At age ten, David went to work in a cotton factory. He worked fourteen-hour days, followed by two hours of night school. But that didn't satisfy his burning desire to learn. He would stay up past midnight studying Latin, science, mathematics, and astronomy. He would prop a book open and read a sentence here and there as he worked.

After putting his trust in Christ, he felt called to missionary work. For several years he saved every penny he could. Then, at the age of twenty-three, he enrolled at a university where he studied about God and medicine and science.

While he was a student, he met Robert Moffat, the missionary pioneer from southern Africa. David was fascinated by him. Moffat said there were thousands of African villages where no missionary had ever been. At that time most Europeans knew very little about the outside edges of Africa and nothing at all about its vast interior (inside).

David became convinced that God was calling him to the "white man's grave," as the African continent was then called. When he finished school, he sailed for Africa.

Soon after he arrived, he set off on an exploratory trip, looking for a place to start his own mission. Wherever he went, he tried to teach the Africans about God and help them in practical ways.

While he lived with the Bakhatla people (which means People of the Monkey), he shot a lion that was eating their cattle and sheep. But his first shot didn't kill the animal. While he was reloading his gun to shoot again, the lion attacked. It sank its teeth into his shoulder and shook him. He would have been killed, but one other man also had a gun, and he shot the lion. It dropped David to charge at the other man, before it finally collapsed.

David became very sick from infection. Moffat's daughter Mary nursed him back to health, but his crushed arm was never the same and caused pain the rest of his life.

Mary later became his wife, and together they started several mission stations. They would move when their water supply dried up. David believed there was better land and more water to the north. He explored hundreds of miles and discovered a beautiful lake. But when he tried to return to the place with his family, their water ran out. They were forced to travel through the desert four days without any water, and Mary and the children became very ill. Their baby girl died. Realizing that his family couldn't endure the hardships he did, David sent them back to England.

He missed his family terribly, but this allowed him to concentrate on exploring more of Africa. He was eager to find fertile land, good water supplies, and rivers to travel on so that other missionaries could come behind him. He also hoped to stop the cruel slave trade by persuading more Europeans to become involved in decent, honest trading with Africans.

His travels were like an endless adventure movie. He narrowly escaped charging buffaloes and elephants, thousand-pound crocodiles, enormous pythons, raging hippopotamuses, and the spears of natives who assumed he was a hated slave trader. Warriors sometimes ran at him waving knives to see what he would do. When he didn't flinch or run, he won their respect and often their friendship as well.

His explorations were as difficult as they were dangerous. In the desert he trudged through blistering heat. In steamy forests he waded through marshes or walked in rain day after day and slept in wet blankets at night. Disease-carrying insects and foul water made him sick again and again. It was more than four years before he got back to England and his family.

When David returned to Africa this time, Mary left the children with friends and relatives and joined him on the Zambezi River. But they were together only three months before Mary died of malaria. He was heartbroken, but he pressed on.

On his next visit home, six years later, David was sick and discouraged. But after a year's rest, he returned once more to Africa, determined to find the source of the Nile River.

His last years were filled with troubles and suffering. All but a faithful few of his crew deserted him. His medicine chest and most of his supplies were stolen. His aging body could no longer endure the hardships and throw off diseases. Yet he refused to stop while Africans were still being sold into misery and dying without hope.

When a reporter named Henry Stanley finally found him, he looked like a living skeleton. His teeth were gone, his eyes were infected, his shoes were in ribbons, and his feet were covered with open sores. Stanley brought healthy food and supplies and stayed for four months. Before he left, he begged the missionary to come home with him, but David felt he couldn't leave with his work unfinished. Although he had to be carried on a stretcher during his final months, he continued to take notes.

During his thirty-two years in Africa, David Livingstone traveled more than 40,000 miles. Within a hundred years of his death, missions and churches had been started all over the vast areas where he had been the first Christian to go. His maps and detailed notes made it much easier for those who followed him. Today, 275 million Africans call themselves Christians.[1]

DISCUSS

We have many opportunities to "plant seeds"—to say or do something that might make a non-Christian start thinking about Jesus. List some ways you have tried to do this or ways you could do so in the future.

38

GEORGE WASHINGTON

EVENING, MORNING AND NOON I CRY OUT IN DIS-
TRESS, AND HE HEARS MY VOICE. HE RANSOMS ME
UNHARMED FROM THE BATTLE WAGED AGAINST ME,
EVEN THOUGH MANY OPPOSE ME. (PSALM 55:17–18)

George Washington's strength of character is well-known, but few history books describe him as the man of prayer that he was. His character, wisdom, and successful leadership were the result of his faithfulness in prayer.

During his childhood in colonial Virginia, George's mother read the Bible to him, taught him to live in a Christian way, and encouraged him to memorize Bible verses. But it was his godly stepbrother, Lawrence, who inspired him most. Lawrence was thirteen years older. When George was eleven, his father died, and Lawrence became like a second father to him.

George Washington had little formal education, but he read a great deal. He studied military books. From Lawrence, who was an adjutant general in the Virginia militia, he learned how to recruit and drill troops. After his brother became ill and resigned from the military, George was appointed to take his place as a major.

When Lawrence died, George spent much time praying. He especially prayed for direction for his life and that he would be able to do God's will in all things. God answered those prayers by using the following difficult years to prepare him for the monumental undertaking he would one day face.

France had moved into English territory in the Ohio River Valley and refused to leave. The French and Indian War that followed dragged on for more than five years. George's life was miraculously spared several times. During one battle, two horses were shot from underneath him. Later, he found four bullet holes in his coat. But his leadership helped England and the colonies win back their land.

After the war, he went home to Virginia. There he married a young widow with two small children and began serving in the state government. He happily settled into daily routines. He read his Bible, he prayed every morning, and he made sure his family attended church faithfully. They entertained guests often. But trouble was brewing.

Wanting to recover the cost of the war, England started charging the colonists heavy taxes on goods they bought from England. (England didn't allow them to trade with other countries.) And, unlike other British citizens, the colonists were not allowed to vote on the way they were taxed. This made them angry.

One thing led to another, and the colonists decided to fight for independence from England. The Continental Congress made George commander in chief of the American army. He knew that without God's help the tiny brand-new nation didn't have a chance against the most powerful empire on earth. He was often found on his knees with an open Bible, asking God for help.

When the fighting started, his army consisted of 16,000 untrained volunteers, armed only with guns they'd brought from home. Two thousand men didn't have guns. None of them had uniforms. He had to identify officers by pinning different colored ribbons on their arms. Many men were poor farmers who didn't have warm clothing or even shoes. To make matters more desperate, Britain had captured much of the colonies' gunpowder.

The new country had no navy, but trading ships helped the army by capturing British ships and giving the supplies to the army. Troops raided British storehouses for guns and gunpowder. Metal statues were melted down to make bullets.

George spent many sleepless nights. He wrote letter after letter to Congress, pleading for more supplies. He also found a chaplain to hold prayer services every morning.

Because the British had taken over Boston, he moved his men into the hills around the city to stop them from going farther into the country. While the British soldiers sat by crackling fires inside Boston homes, George's troops huddled against winter winds in tents in the snow. Before they attacked, he asked his men to fast and pray.

God answered prayer in a marvelous way. While one group of men fired cannons to distract the British, the rest of them moved closer and quickly built rough forts. Then a heavy fog set in, just in time to keep them out of sight. At the same time, British ships sailing toward the harbor were blown the other direction by a hurricane-force wind. When the British commander in Boston saw that they were surrounded, he surrendered.

The next major battle was in New York. Britain had 5,000 ships and 32,000 men. George had no ships and half that many men. After fighting three days, he began to retreat until the river was at their backs. If the British caught up with them, all would be lost. During the night, he borrowed barges to quietly move his troops across the river. A swift wind began to blow and sped them on their way. Only three men were left to be captured when the British arrived the next morning. George knew God had sent the wind to save them in time.

The colonists won battles at Trenton and Princeton but lost the next two. The British forces took over Philadelphia, the American capital at the time. George didn't have enough supplies to attack, so he moved his troops to Valley Forge, a hilltop twenty miles away, to wait for more.

It is doubtful that he and his men would have made it through the hard winter at Valley Forge without God's help. The soldiers slept in tents until they built log huts. They didn't have enough food or clothing. One thousand men didn't have shoes. When they went from tent to tent, they left bloody footprints in the snow. George often went to a nearby grove of trees to ask God to give them strength. But the supplies finally came, and the long winter ended.

France decided to help the American soldiers. George and his men surrounded the British at Yorktown, and French ships stopped them from escaping by sea. They were forced to surrender. The Americans collected many guns. A year and one-half later, the war ended. It had lasted more than seven years.

George was thrilled to be back at home, but there was more work for him to do. In 1787, he met with leaders from other states to write a constitution. When they finished, the representatives unanimously elected George to be the first president of the United States of America. He didn't want the job, but he agreed to take it.

Leading a brand-new country was frightening. There were many different opinions about how the country should be run and how much power the national government should have. George prayerfully worked out fair solutions and kept peace between all the groups.

When his four-year term was over, he was eager to go home, but everyone wanted him to serve another four years. After a second term, he was asked to serve again, but George declined and went home to Virginia. He died a few years later.

DISCUSS

Do you believe praying is the most important thing you can do? Why? Does the amount of time you spend in prayer prove you feel that way?

39
JOHN TESTRAKE

GOD IS OUR REFUGE AND STRENGTH, AN
EVER-PRESENT HELP IN TROUBLE. THEREFORE WE
WILL NOT FEAR, THOUGH THE EARTH GIVE WAY AND
THE MOUNTAINS FALL INTO THE HEART OF THE SEA.

(PSALM 46:1–2)

In June 1985, TWA pilot John Testrake left home for what he thought would be a routine flight to Rome. Kissing his wife good-bye, he mentioned the anniversary cruise they were planning to take in five days.

But John and his wife didn't go on that cruise, because TWA Flight 847 was not a routine flight. A few minutes after takeoff, there was a banging in the passenger cabin. His flight engineer got up and looked through the peephole in the door separating the cockpit from the cabin. When he came back, he told John, "We've got a hijack."

The hijackers were two young, nervous, Arabic-speaking men, heavily armed with guns and hand grenades. They burst into the cockpit, aimed a gun at John, and demanded that the plane head for Algiers on the coast of North Africa. He tried to explain that the plane didn't have enough fuel to go that far, but the men spoke very little English. They kept yelling, "Algiers!"

Finally, one of the crew discovered that the hijackers understood some German and was able to tell the men they had to stop for fuel. The hijackers agreed to stop at Beirut, Lebanon. On the way, they ran up and down the aisles, hitting passengers and some of the crew with the butts of their guns. They also severely beat a young American soldier.

As John was landing the plane in Beirut, one of the men held a shaking pistol to the back of his neck and a grenade in front of his face. He knew the men were radical Muslims, who believed they would earn a special reward in paradise for dying for their beliefs. Yet he felt a strange calmness. He knew he was in God's hands.

He had been through hard times before and had learned to lean on the Lord. He had lost an infant son in an auto accident that nearly killed him too. His first wife had died of cancer. Not long after he remarried, his oldest son had suddenly died.

Having a strong personal relationship with Christ, John wasn't afraid to die. But that didn't mean he wasn't deeply concerned about the safety of the 145 passengers and his crew. His faith helped him think clearly and talk calmly to the hijackers.

He learned that they intended to hold the plane and passengers for ransom. They would exchange them only if the United States pressured Israel into releasing some Lebanese hostages whom Israel was holding.

The plane was refueled, some passengers were allowed off, and they headed to Algiers. When the hijackers' demands weren't granted, the plane was refueled again, and they flew back to Beirut. Again the hijackers didn't get the answers they wanted. Deciding to prove they were deadly serious, they shot the soldier that had earlier been beaten and threw his body out of the plane.

More hijackers came on board. John was forced to fly back to Algiers. Then back to Beirut. This time he and his flight engineer convinced the hijackers that something was wrong with the plane and they couldn't go anywhere else.

The remaining passengers were taken off the plane and held elsewhere. But during the next two weeks, John, his flight engineer, and his first officer waited out the negotiations aboard the parked plane under the watchful eyes of a dozen guards.

The new guards seemed calmer and more levelheaded than the original hijackers, though. They were curious when John and his flight engineer, also a Christian, prayed and sang hymns together and read the Bible.

Finally, seventeen days after he'd left home, John, his crew, and the passengers were reunited and released. Millions of Americans who had followed the ordeal on the nightly news considered him a hero, whose cool head and strong faith had kept a very dangerous situation from becoming more tragic.

During press conferences following their release, he took the opportunity to witness to God's faithfulness, saying that the thing he remembered most about the experience was the constant presence of Jesus. He explained that Christ had comforted him, kept him from being afraid, and given him hope.

John continued to fly for TWA until his retirement. Then he piloted planes for Mission Aviation Fellowship, delivering supplies to missionaries in remote parts of the world. In 1994, he became chairman of Missouri's Christian Coalition, a Christian group that works for change using the political system. He died of cancer at the age of sixty-eight.

DISCUSS

Think of a difficult time you've gone through. Did Christ's presence seem real to you at the time? How aware of His presence are you on a typical day? Is there anything you can say or do that will remind you of His closeness?

40

EDITH SCHAEFFER

OFFER HOSPITALITY TO ONE ANOTHER
WITHOUT GRUMBLING. (1 PETER 4:9)

While World War Two raged in Europe, Edith Schaeffer helped her husband, Francis, pastor a growing church in Missouri. Francis and Edith felt truly blessed. Their congregation loved them, and Edith especially enjoyed working with the children in the church. At the same time, they couldn't keep from worrying about all of the Christians suffering throughout Europe.

They were not alone in their concern. When the war ended, a group of churches asked Francis to go to Europe and see how Christians in the bombed cities were doing. He came home to report that many European pastors no longer even claimed to be Bible-believing Christians. He was deeply concerned that many churches were turning their backs on the old Christian beliefs and were watering down what the Bible said. Then his church denomination asked Francis and his family to become missionaries to Europe. They also wanted the Schaeffers to start the International Council of Christian Churches to fight the new liberal ideas.

The Schaeffers agreed, but Edith wondered what one family could accomplish on a continent where people were discouraged and exhausted from such a terrible war. How could they inspire Europeans to faith and challenge them to battle for truth when they desperately longed for peace and rest?

Their first years in Europe were anything but easy. Edith and the children lived in tiny, shabby apartments while Francis traveled and spoke. At other times, the whole family lived like nomads, traveling from country to country. Francis and Edith tirelessly started Bible classes and camps for boys and girls. They wrote Bible studies for adults and children and sent them all over Europe.

No matter how busy they were, though, they never missed an opportunity to help those around them—soldiers, students, villagers. Because of their warmth, hospitality, and openness, people started coming to them to ask questions about Christianity.

This sometimes got them into trouble. In 1955, they were told they would have to leave their home in Switzerland after a local leader became a Christian through their influence. The Roman Catholic authorities did not want people to leave their church to become evangelicals. The news came at a stressful time. Their young son, Franky, had come down with polio and was severely paralyzed. Their daughter Susan had rheumatic fever. (Both children later recovered.)

The Schaeffers had three days to make an appeal. They also had to prove they had made a financial arrangement to rent or buy a house. Their house hunting was interrupted by a couple who needed their help. The wife was about to have a baby. With time running out, the Schaeffers hated to delay their house search, but they did.

As soon as the baby was born, Edith went out in the middle of a snowstorm, again looking for a home. When she was told what the house she'd just looked at would cost per month, she started to cry. It was much more than they could afford, and there was only one hour left before the deadline. While she walked on with tear-filled eyes, a realtor stopped her. The woman told her about a cottage for sale in a Protestant state.

As soon as Edith saw that house, she knew it was God's answer, and she trusted that He would provide the money for the down payment. She prayed that somehow He would send $1,000 before ten o'clock the next day. The next morning, a letter came with a check for $1,000. The papers were filled out just in time.

Shortly after they moved into their new home, Edith's daughter Priscilla called to ask if she could bring a wealthy college classmate home for the weekend. Edith was tempted to say no. The chalet was far from ready for company. The woodstove smoked. The furnace didn't work. Many boxes were still left to be unpacked. But when Priscilla said the girl had been studying different religions and was confused about what to believe, she agreed. She did her best to welcome their guest, prepare delightful meals, and lovingly explain the truth about Christ.

The weekend proved to be a turning point in the Schaeffers' ministry. Word got out in the local university that they would welcome anyone and answer any honest questions about God. Many students started coming to their home. They named their home *L'Abri,* which is French for "the Shelter." It became an international study center where people from all over the world came to learn about God. Edith and Francis were highly skilled at explaining their faith in a logical, convincing way. But proving they were right was never as important as treating every guest in a loving way.

Edith made every person who came to their home feel special. Franky recalls the day the United States ambassador to Switzerland was waiting for tea in their living room. His father sent him to see why his mother was taking so long. When Franky walked into the kitchen, he found his mother comforting a sobbing teenage girl in a filthy T-shirt and threadbare jeans.

The girl had been talking about killing herself. She was part of the hippie movement of the late 1960s and had been hitchhiking across Europe with a boyfriend who'd left her, pregnant and hooked on hard drugs. As Edith stroked the girl's greasy hair, she assured her that God still loved her.

The ambassador eventually got his tea and fresh-baked oatmeal cookies. He asked the Schaeffers many questions about how Christianity fit into modern times and ideas. Like the weeping girl in the kitchen, he received patient, gentle answers.

Edith lovingly shared her time, her home, and her faith with thousands of students, professors, and pastors—anyone who came seeking answers about God. Eventually, L'Abri branches were started in other countries. Both Francis and Edith wrote books that sold millions of copies. He died in 1984, but she continues to work with L'Abri.

Discuss

Describe a time when someone changed his or her plans for you. How did that make you feel? How flexible are you to interruptions from others?

41

JOHN NEWTON

HAVE NOTHING TO DO WITH THE FRUITLESS DEEDS OF
DARKNESS, BUT RATHER EXPOSE THEM. . . . EVERY-
THING EXPOSED BY THE LIGHT BECOMES VISIBLE, FOR
IT IS LIGHT THAT MAKES EVERYTHING VISIBLE.

(EPHESIANS 5:11, 13–14)

John Newton was born in England in 1725 to a godly mother and a sea captain father. He started going to sea when he was nine. By the time he was fourteen, he could handle a ship as well as any grown man. Then his mother died, and his father remarried. John no longer felt wanted at home. Filled with bitterness, he turned his back on God.

Wanting to be alone one night, he went for a long walk and stopped in a bar. A navy officer and some soldiers followed him when he left. They hit him on the head, carried him to a ship, and threw him into the hold.

At the time, men were often forced into the English navy in this way. John learned that the ship he was on would be gone for five years, and he tried to escape. He was soon caught, though, and thrown back into the hold. A week later he was convicted of desertion and sentenced to be beaten eight dozen times with a tough leather whip.

Before his wounds had time to heal, he was forced to work. The brutal punishment filled him with hatred, and he dreamed of killing the captain. Then one day he was traded for a sailor on another ship.

He found he had been moved to a slave ship. In those days, most people in England thought buying and selling slaves was a respectable business. At first he was horrified to see how cruelly the slaves were treated. But after he heard how much money the slave trader had made in a short time, he wanted to work for him.

The trader, Amos Clow, made a bargain with the ship's captain to let him go. Amos liked John very much until another slave trader stole some of his things and blamed John. Then Amos made John his slave and treated him badly.

And then, yet another slave trader talked Amos into letting John come to work for him. This trader treated him well and helped him become rather wealthy. John became very proud. He drank, swore, and often made fun of religious people.

But when his ship got caught in a terrible storm, he wasn't so sure of himself. He was afraid of drowning, and he tried to remember what his mother had taught him about the Bible. The ship survived the storm, but it was badly damaged and most of its food supply was lost. Five days passed before the desperate crew spotted land. John finally got to shore and went to a church, where he told God he was sorry for his sin and asked Jesus to come into his heart.

Now that he was a Christian, he made changes in his life. He stopped swearing and drinking. He started treating his slaves and crew with more kindness. He also married a sweet girl he had known since his youth.

His eyes were opened to how wrong slavery was while he was on a three-year slave trading trip. A man who had just bought ten slave boys said he planned to work them as rough and hard as he could—until they had to be replaced with a new load. Seeing the terror on the faces of the young boys, John felt as if he had killed them himself. Later, the sobbing and moaning of the slaves in their quarters haunted him. He knew he could no longer be a part of the slave trade.

He returned home and found a job inspecting and taxing ships. In his free time he read the best Christian books available. Although he had quit school at eleven, he now studied Greek and Hebrew so that he could understand the Bible better. He was often asked to share his life's story, and he soon overcame his natural shyness. When friends suggested that he become a pastor, he agreed.

John's heart was filled with wonder and gratitude that God had forgiven him for his sins and all the pain he had caused others. He expressed his deep gratitude in a beautiful hymn he wrote, which has touched people ever since—"Amazing Grace."

For forty-three years John served as a loving pastor. He spoke out on the evils of the slave trade and wrote a book about the brutality he had seen. He persuaded William Wilberforce, a popular lawmaker in England, to wage war on the sickening business, until a law was finally passed to stop it.

The former slave trader also helped start two worldwide missionary societies. These groups took the Good News that sets men free to the very parts of Africa where John had enslaved so many.

DISCUSS

After John Newton realized how wrong slavery was, he did everything he could to stop it. Have you ever tried to stop a wrong? When? Is there something going on around you that you feel God wants you to speak out against?

42

LEANN THIEMAN

"FOR I KNOW THE PLANS I HAVE FOR YOU,"
DECLARES THE LORD, "PLANS TO PROSPER YOU
AND NOT TO HARM YOU, PLANS TO GIVE YOU
HOPE AND A FUTURE." (JEREMIAH 29:11)

LeAnn Thieman was an Iowa housewife and part-time nurse with two young daughters. It was 1975, and on the other side of the world the Vietnam War dragged on, leaving more than a million children orphans. LeAnn was an officer in an organization that raised money to help those orphans by arranging adoptions in the United States. She and her husband had also applied to adopt a Vietnamese baby themselves.

Although she had rarely been out of the Midwest, LeAnn agreed to make a trip to Saigon, the capital of South Vietnam. She planned to bring back a half-dozen babies. The situation in Vietnam seemed fairly stable. No fighting was going on near Saigon. Her close friend, Carol Dey, who also volunteered for Friends of Children of Vietnam, decided to go with her.

But in the months between their promise to go and the date they were to leave, things changed drastically. North Vietnam, the Communist country trying to take over South Vietnam, began an all-out attack. In a short time the South Vietnamese president surrendered a fourth of his country to the advancing Communists. Days before the women planned to leave, the fighting and bombing moved dangerously close to Saigon.

LeAnn and Carol listened to news reports and predictions that the whole country would soon fall to the Communists, and they were filled with fear. What if they got caught in the middle of combat? What if the Communists—who hated Americans—captured them and held them as prisoners? What if they never came home?

In church on Easter Sunday, LeAnn's heart was in total turmoil. Was it fair to her husband and children to take such a risk? After the church service ended, she sat alone in the empty building, crying and praying. And then she began to relax. A feeling of well-being and courage came over her. She became convinced that God wanted her to go to Vietnam and that He would take care of her. That calmness stayed even when she heard a report of bombing just three miles from Saigon.

Carol, on the other hand, was a bundle of anxiety as they began their journey. By the time the plane stopped in Guam, the worry had made her sick. Deeply concerned, LeAnn unselfishly urged her friend to head back to the States. But Carol decided to keep going.

On the flight from Guam to Manila, a flight attendant told Carol that going in spite of her fears showed incredible courage. He spoke about the opportunity they had to change lives forever and assured her that she could be strong enough. After talking to him, Carol was like a different person and shared LeAnn's confidence about the trip. The two women later wondered if the man had been God's special messenger.

They finally landed in Saigon, and a woman who worked for their organization told them President Ford had okayed a giant baby-lift. That meant that, instead of taking back a half-dozen babies, they would take nearly two hundred with them. LeAnn was thrilled and believed this was the reason God had drawn her to come.

The walls at the orphanage were lined with cribs. Mats with babies on them covered the floors. Workers were busy around the clock trying to get out as many orphans as they could before Vietnam fell. (Many of the babies were half-American and would be treated badly if left behind.) LeAnn and Carol worked tirelessly caring for babies and getting paperwork ready.

Then another group was allowed to take their place on a flight out of Saigon, for the danger was quickly mounting. LeAnn was crushed. Her frustration changed to horror, though, when that same plane crashed shortly after takeoff. Officials thought someone had purposely damaged it.

The delay brought another surprise. Because arranging an adoption normally took a year, she didn't expect to bring her own child home. It had only been a few weeks since she and her husband mailed their application. But as conditions became desperate in South Vietnam, the adoption process was greatly speeded up. LeAnn was told she could choose her own son from the babies at the center. She realized this was yet another reason she had known she had to come.

While she looked at all the precious babies, wondering how she could choose, a baby boy crawled to her. When she picked him up, he cuddled on her shoulder and babbled happily. She prayed about her decision as she held him. Then, with tears of joy, she introduced their new son, Mitchell Thieman, to her friends.

There were several more nerve-shattering delays and then a frenzied rush to the airport. Finally, LeAnn, Carol, and Mitchell sat on a plane filled with babies. Remembering the aircraft that had crashed, LeAnn prayed fervently as the plane lifted off the ground. She was overwhelmed with gratitude and relief when the captain announced that they were out of range of the Communists.

Once they landed in the United States, other volunteers escorted the babies to their new homes. One week after leaving Iowa, LeAnn returned—weak, exhausted, and thrilled to be home with her son.

DISCUSS

Have you ever felt God urging you to do something? What? Did you do it? How can we learn to "hear" His urges better?

43
HENRIETTA MEARS

Now to him who is able to do immeasurably
more than all we ask or imagine, according
to his power that is at work within us, to
him be glory in the church and in Christ
Jesus throughout all generations, for
ever and ever! Amen. (Ephesians 3:20–21)

From the time she was six years old, Henrietta Mears had very poor eyesight. But that didn't stop her from seeing all she could do for God.

She was born into a happy, wealthy family in Fargo, North Dakota. Her father owned twenty banks. Her mother was a deeply committed Christian who prayed an hour every morning and gave New Testaments to salesmen who came to their door.

Even as a child, Henrietta was eager to learn all she could about God and begged to go along to adult church meetings. She trusted in Christ as her Savior when she was seven, and she taught her first Sunday school class at the age of eleven. During high school, she hoped to become a missionary and was disappointed when she realized that wasn't God's plan for her life.

Her sight became weaker as she grew older and got even worse when she accidentally jabbed one of her eyes with a hat pin. After high school, her doctors advised her not to go on for more schooling. If she did, they predicted, she would be blind by the time she was thirty.

But Henrietta said she would study as hard as she could for as long as she could. In college, she taught herself to listen carefully in class so that she wouldn't have to spend as much time reading.

When she graduated from college, she started teaching high school chemistry and a young people's Bible class in a small town in Minnesota. Later, she moved to a bigger school in Minneapolis, and there she went door to door, inviting young women to her Sunday school class. She started with fifty-five students. Within ten years the number had grown to more than five hundred.

In 1928, the pastor of First Presbyterian Church in Hollywood asked Henrietta to become the church's Director of Christian Education. She agreed and dreamed of building a Sunday school that truly changed lives.

She believed the Bible would draw young people like a magnet if it was taught the way it should be. She worked hard to make sure that every lesson was excellent and the teachers were well trained. When she went to First Presbyterian, there were 450 students in the Sunday school. Two and a half years later there were 4,200. Parents traveled as much as fifty miles to bring their children.

But Henrietta was upset with the Sunday school materials the church used. She looked for something better. Not finding any as exciting as she thought they should be, she set out to write her own. Her exceptional lessons touched many students' lives.

Soon people from other churches asked for copies. Eventually, Henrietta started Gospel Light Publications and, along with other writers, wrote lessons for all twelve grades. By 1937, more than a quarter million of her Sunday school books had been sold.

She taught the church's college-age class herself. She was a fun-loving person with a great sense of humor. She wore fancy hats and painted her car canary yellow and kelly green because her college boys liked it flashy. Always available for counseling, she personally led thousands to Christ. Her students loved her, and in turn she taught them to love the Lord.

Henrietta taught young people to look into the future and dream of great tomorrows. During her time at First Presbyterian, more than four hundred of her students decided to go into Christian work full-time. Quite a few of them became well-known Christian leaders, such as Bill Bright, who started Campus Crusade.

One of her many gifts was recognizing and encouraging others' potential. She once invited a young, little-known evangelist named Billy Graham to speak at a conference held at her church's camp. At the time, Billy was wrestling with doubts about some of the things the Bible said. He shared his struggles with Henrietta, but she continued to believe in him and pray for him.

The time Billy spent at that camp proved to be a turning point in his life. One night as he wandered through the woods praying, he decided he would accept the entire Bible as true. He realized it didn't matter if it all made sense to him. It was God's Word, and he would believe it.

When he spoke the next day, Henrietta knew something was different. His message was powerful and convincing. Four hundred young people gave their lives to Christ after he finished. Soon after that, he held an extremely successful crusade and became a well-known evangelist. Years later, Billy said that no woman beside his mother and his wife had influenced him as much as Henrietta had.

Henrietta Mears died in 1963. She never became a missionary, but she taught others who touched more lives than she ever could have on her own. Many consider her the most influential woman in modern church history.

DISCUSS

Consider this statement: "Our plans are often too small to require God's miraculous power." Have you ever dreamed of God's doing something BIG through you? What? Consider your natural abilities, talents, and interests. Think of some ways God could use them to make a difference.

44
MARTIN LUTHER

I AM NOT ASHAMED OF THE GOSPEL, BECAUSE IT IS
THE POWER OF GOD FOR THE SALVATION OF EVERY-
ONE WHO BELIEVES: FIRST FOR THE JEW, THEN FOR
THE GENTILE. FOR IN THE GOSPEL A RIGHTEOUSNESS
FROM GOD IS REVEALED, A RIGHTEOUSNESS THAT IS
BY FAITH FROM FIRST TO LAST, JUST AS IT IS
WRITTEN: "THE RIGHTEOUS WILL LIVE BY FAITH."

(ROMANS 1:16–17)

In 1483, a baby was born in a small German village who would one day change the history of Christianity and the world. He was named Martin Luther. As Martin grew, his father was proud of how quickly he learned. Since Mr. Luther was a poor miner, he wanted his son to get an education and have a better life than he had. When Martin was eighteen, his father sent him to the university to become a lawyer.

But Martin was more interested in finding answers about God. Ever since he was a young boy, he had been afraid of dying and facing God's eternal punishment. He desperately wanted to know what he could do to win God's love.

One day he was walking through a forest when a bolt of lightning struck so close that it knocked him down. Terrified, Martin promised to become a monk so that he could be sure of earning his way to heaven. (A monk is someone who spends all of his time trying to get to know God better.)

As a monk, Martin did many things to prove his devotion to God. He went without eating for days at a time. He slept on a narrow wooden plank without any blankets in an unheated room. Every day he confessed his sins to a priest and asked for forgiveness. Yet he was overwhelmed with feelings of guilt. He tried, but he never felt good enough to earn God's love.

Because Martin was so intelligent, he was chosen to go back to school to become a teacher. Then he was assigned to teach the Bible, a subject that had never been taught before at the University of Wittenberg.

While he was teaching from the book of Romans, Martin found the answer he had been searching for all of his life. God would forgive him for every sin he had ever done if he trusted in Jesus Christ alone to save him.

It was as if a huge weight had been lifted off his shoulders. He was overcome with joy and couldn't wait to share the good news with his students. Soon large crowds were coming to hear him because they had never heard God's Word taught so clearly.

At the time there were few Bibles, and those were printed in Latin, which most people couldn't read. On top of that, there was only one kind of church—Roman Catholic. It had many rules people were told to follow in order to get God's blessing. It taught that people who died went to a place called purgatory, where their souls were made pure so they could go on to heaven.

Several actions were supposed to bring God's forgiveness: (1) you could buy a letter of forgiveness from a priest, (2) you could pray to an important Christian who had died, asking him to ask Christ to forgive you, or (3) you could touch some object from a great Christian who had died, such as a bone or piece of clothing.

The Roman Catholic Church was very powerful then. The government punished anyone who dared to disagree with its teachings. But Martin wanted everyone to know the truth about getting sins forgiven, so he wrote ninety-five statements about what the Bible really said. He nailed the list to the door of a large church. He did so on a special day when thousands were in Wittenberg.

News of what he had written spread like wildfire. Printers made copies, and people all over Germany began talking about what he had said. The church leaders and the king who ruled Germany became very angry. They ordered Martin to appear before them.

At the hearing, they told Martin to make a public statement that he had been wrong. He refused. Back then, anyone who disobeyed the church that way was burned at the stake. But Martin had an important friend, a German prince. The Spanish king didn't want to make the prince angry by killing Martin, because the king needed the prince's help in the war with France. The king let him go, but he declared he was "outside the law," which meant that anyone who killed him would not be punished.

On his way home, a band of men on horses stopped Martin's wagon. They covered his head and dragged him into the woods. As soon as they were away from the road, they told him they were friends, and they took him to an abandoned castle to hide.

While most people thought he was dead, Martin Luther was safe in the castle, translating the New Testament into German so that everyone could read it. Later, he wrote books explaining Christianity. He also wrote many beautiful hymns such as "A Mighty Fortress Is Our God." After he dared to come out of hiding, he married and had children. They welcomed daily guests who came to learn more about the Christian faith. Then Martin and others translated the Old Testament too.

Martin Luther's teachings and the German Bibles persuaded many to break away from the Roman church. When church leaders tried to make them come back, his followers wrote a formal "protest." Because of this, they came to be known as Protestants, a name still used today for non-Catholic Christians.

DISCUSS

Most people in America consider themselves Christians. But not all of them understand what it means to be saved. What wrong ideas do some people have? How can we answer them?

45
AMY CARMICHAEL

THE SPIRIT HIMSELF TESTIFIES WITH OUR SPIRIT
THAT WE ARE GOD'S CHILDREN. NOW IF WE ARE
CHILDREN, THEN WE ARE HEIRS—HEIRS OF GOD
AND CO-HEIRS WITH CHRIST, IF INDEED WE SHARE
IN HIS SUFFERINGS IN ORDER THAT WE MAY ALSO
SHARE IN HIS GLORY. (ROMANS 8:16–17)

When Amy Carmichael was a girl, her father gave her advice that guided the rest of her life: "Never give in to difficulty."

Amy was born in 1867 to a well-to-do Christian family in Northern Ireland. Her days were spent swimming, riding horses, and studying with governesses at home. Whenever she thought one of her governesses was too strict, mischievous Amy made her life miserable until she quit.

At thirteen, Amy went away to boarding school, where she accepted Christ. After her father died, she became committed to serving God wherever she could. She held children's meetings, taught night school in the slums, visited homes witnessing, started a schoolgirls' prayer meeting, and volunteered at the YWCA.

She also held special church services for factory girls. Those services soon outgrew the church building, and Amy prayed for money to build a bigger hall. The money soon came from a wealthy lady who had heard of her work. The new hall, named The Welcome, was open seven days a week and offered many different kinds of meetings and classes.

By the time Amy was twenty, her father's savings were gone. A friend offered her family a home and work in England, where Amy started another ministry like The Welcome. She worked so hard that her health grew worse and worse until neuralgia, a disease of the nerves that made her whole body ache, forced her to rest.

She recuperated at the home of an elderly friend she called the Dear Old Man. Amy now felt that God wanted her to become a missionary, but her mind was torn. She knew she wasn't very healthy, and she thought both her mother and the Dear Old Man needed her. But they both encouraged her to follow God's leading, so Amy applied to a mission board to serve in China.

Turned down because of physical weakness, she went to Japan instead. She worked there fifteen months before the rainy weather made her ill. When the Dear Old Man had a stroke, she went back to England.

Amy was twenty-eight when she left her mother, the Dear Old Man, and her home for the last time and headed for India. Once she got there, she was weighed down with home-sickness and loneliness. The heat—often 100 to 110 degrees in the shade—exhausted her, the scenery was dull, and she had no close friends.

Life in India could be cruel. A million people a year died of malaria. Unwanted baby girls were sometimes killed. Widows were often burned with their dead husbands' bodies. Indians who accepted Christ were often threatened, beaten, drugged, or killed. Indians were born into certain social classes—or castes—and could not move up or down, no matter what they did. People from different castes could not even associate with each other.

India's Hindu religion was complicated and confusing. Cows were considered holy. They couldn't be eaten even if people were starving. People thought it was wrong to kill an insect, because it might be a dead relative come back to life.

But Amy wouldn't give up. She gathered a group of Christian Indian women called "The Starry Cluster" to travel with her and teach women and children about Jesus.

One day a girl named Preena asked Amy to help her. Her poor mother had given her to the temple, where she was shamefully abused as men worshiped the false gods. She had run away once before, and her hands had been branded with hot irons.

Amy couldn't believe the terrible stories Preena told about how young girls were treated in the temple. She disguised herself and sneaked into the temple to investigate. What she learned horrified her. From then on, she was always ready to rescue a child about to be given or sold to a temple.

Sometimes she and her helper traveled many miles in extreme heat only to get to a village too late. Her life was threatened many, many times. If caught helping a child escape, she could be charged with kidnapping and put in prison.

Runaways and abandoned children also came to her. Soon she was too busy caring for them to go out preaching and teaching. Within ten years she had two hundred youngsters in her care. She was a fun-filled guardian who loved to play, but her heart ached for the thousands she couldn't help. By the end of her life, she had cared for almost one thousand boys and girls—many of whom spread God's message throughout India.

As Amy's work grew, she prayed for more helpers, more land, and more buildings—and God answered. She wrote a book telling about the terrible ways temple children were treated. Many people were shocked when they read it, and laws were passed to stop the abuse.

Then she became crippled after a bad fall. She rarely left her room during the last twenty years of her life and was never without pain. Yet Amy continued to oversee the orphanage and write books. In all, she wrote thirty-five books and many beautiful poems.

DISCUSS

One of Amy's poems says:

No wound? No scar?
Yet as the Master shall the servant be,

And pierced are the feet that follow Me;
But thine are whole: can he have followed far
Who has no wound or scar?[1]

Do you have any "wounds" or "scars" from following Jesus? Are there any ways being a Christian has made your life harder?

46

JIM ELLIOT

I TELL YOU THE TRUTH, UNLESS A KERNEL OF WHEAT
FALLS TO THE GROUND AND DIES, IT REMAINS ONLY A
SINGLE SEED. BUT IF IT DIES, IT PRODUCES MANY
SEEDS. THE MAN WHO LOVES HIS LIFE WILL LOSE IT,
WHILE THE MAN WHO HATES HIS LIFE IN THIS WORLD
WILL KEEP IT FOR ETERNAL LIFE. (JOHN 12:24–25)

Jim Elliot was a champion wrestler, honor student, amateur poet, and class representative on the student council when he was a student at Wheaton College in Illinois. He was also a young man eager to go wherever and do whatever God asked him to.

Since he planned to become a missionary, Jim studied Greek, the original language of the New Testament, so that he'd be able to translate it into different languages. During his third year of college, he became attracted to another student, Elisabeth Howard, who was also going into mission work.

Jim graduated, then took a year to decide where he should go. The more he learned about a Stone Age tribe in Ecuador known as the Aucas, the more he believed God wanted him to go to them.

No one had ever told the Aucas about Jesus. They lived deep in the Amazon jungle and were cruel man hunters who killed anyone who came into their territory. They especially hated white men. That was because rubber hunters had come to the jungle in the 1800s and burned Auca homes and took their people as slaves.

Jim knew the dangers involved, but he was still eager to take the Good News to the Aucas. His love for God and his desire to reach others for Christ were more important to him than his own life. He went to Ecuador and lived at a mission station called Shandia among the gentle Quichua Indians. He and another missionary set about learning the Quichua language in order to teach them about God. They also built a simple house, a school, and a church and cleared a strip of land for the mission plane to land on.

After he was settled, he married Elisabeth and brought her back to Shandia. They were very happy. Several other missionary couples were working in nearby stations. The Quichua people became their friends, many accepted Christ, and Jim and Elisabeth were soon blessed with a healthy daughter.

He still couldn't forget the Aucas, though. When he heard of an Auca woman who had run away from the tribe and was working nearby as a servant, he hurried to meet her. She taught him some Auca words. And he was thrilled when the missionary pilot discovered a small Auca village from the air.

During the next three months, Jim and the other missionaries often flew over the Auca area. Each time, they lowered gifts tied to a rope—a kettle, flashlight, shirts, candy, beads and buttons, pictures of the missionaries. Using a loudspeaker, they shouted simple Auca sentences such as: "I like you! I am your friend!"

After a while the Indians started tying their own gifts to the rope, and the missionaries thought it was time to try to meet them. Jim and four other men landed near a river in Auca territory. They built a tree house to sleep in, camped out on the beach, and waited for visitors.

A few days later, a young Auca man and two women came out of the jungle. The missionaries gave them some knives and a model airplane and served them hamburgers and lemonade. The three natives spent several hours with them. The man even rode in the airplane and called out to his friends as they flew over Auca homes.

Jim and the others were overjoyed over their first contact with the Indians and looked forward to their next meeting. The following day, the excited missionaries radioed their wives that they had spotted a group of men heading toward their camp.

Back home, the women waited anxiously for a report of the second Auca meeting. But no message came. The missionaries had been ambushed and killed with wooden spears. The people Jim had prayed for for six years killed him along with his four friends.

To some it seemed a senseless waste of a promising young life. But the story of Jim's unselfish devotion inspired many to give their lives more completely to God. Some of those people became well-known Christian leaders, including Chuck Swindoll and Josh McDowell. Many others were stirred to go into mission work after reading about him.

The work Jim Elliot began among the Aucas continued. In 1992, the Auca Indians received the New Testament in their own language. Many Aucas have become Christians, including the five who killed the missionaries.

DISCUSS

Jim Elliot once said, "He is no fool who gives what he cannot keep to gain what he cannot lose." What do you think he meant by that? Think of the things that matter most to you. Which ones are you absolutely sure you will have forever?

47

TOM LANDRY

A FOOL GIVES FULL VENT TO HIS ANGER, BUT A WISE
MAN KEEPS HIMSELF UNDER CONTROL. (PROVERBS 29:11)

Even as a barefoot kid playing football in a small Texas town, Tom Landry showed signs of the kind of coach he would one day become. Whenever someone told another kid he couldn't play because he was small or uncoordinated, Tom told him he could be on his team. "You can do it," he'd quietly tell the boy. "Don't let anyone tell you different."[1]

In high school, Tom was a star football player, his class president, and a member of the National Honor Society. Yet he was unusually modest. If his parents didn't watch one of his games, they never knew how well he did unless they read about it in the newspaper or someone else told them.

Tom received a football scholarship to the University of Texas, but he left college to become an air force pilot during World War Two. He flew thirty combat missions through antiaircraft fire and saw many planes go down. He had a close call himself. In the middle of heavy fog, his plane ran out of gas. He was forced to crash-land, but he and the crew were unharmed.

At the war's end, he returned to the university. After being away from football several years, he had to work extrahard, but he became an outstanding player once again. Despite a nonstop schedule, he found time to fall in love with a beautiful student named Alicia.

The 1949 Orange Bowl was his last college game. He ran 117 yards, and the New York Giants offered him a $6,000 contract. Tom was thrilled. With the $500 signing bonus, he and Alicia could get married.

As a professional player, he made up for whatever he lacked in speed with hard work and keen insight. He spent hours looking at films of other teams and learned to predict other players' moves to give himself a head start.

Tom became a player-coach at the age of twenty-nine because of his ability to predict what teams would do and then plan effective plays. In 1956, he became a full-time defensive coach and helped the Giants win the championship.

By the time he reached his midthirties, he had done everything he'd ever wanted to do in football. But he still felt something was missing. He knew he was at a crossroads but didn't know which way to go. During this time, a friend invited him to a men's Bible study. He agreed to go but only because he couldn't think of a nice way to say no.

Tom had gone to church all of his life, but he had never studied the Bible before. Now that he did, he realized that living a good life wasn't enough. He needed to have his own relationship with Christ. After he came to faith in Jesus, his priorities changed. God became first, his family second, and football third. This focus would help him remain calm through the incredible pressures he would face in the future.

In 1960, he moved to a brand-new team called the Dallas Cowboys. He was the youngest head coach in the league, and he faced the tremendous challenge of starting a professional football team from scratch. Because the Cowboys hadn't been organized when the draft was held in November, he would have no draft picks the first season.

With the odds stacked against them, the Cowboys' record that first year was eleven losses and one tie. It was the worst record any NFL team had had in eighteen years. But Tom wasn't discouraged. He knew it would take three years to build a strong team, and he had a five-year contract. Fellow Texans weren't as patient. They started calling for a new coach.

By the Cowboys' fourth year, the criticism had grown louder. At the end of the season, their four-year record was thirteen wins, three ties, and thirty-eight losses. Through it all, Tom never took his stress out on the players or referees. In fact, he became well-known as a coach who kept his cool during tense times.

Over the next few years, Tom tried many ideas that had never been used before, including picking college players based on an elaborate computer ranking. After a six-year struggle, the tide started to turn, and in 1966 the Cowboys won the Eastern Conference.

The next few years were disappointing, though. No matter how well they did during regular seasons, the Cowboys lost in the play-offs or the championship games. Reporters and fans blamed Tom, saying his Christianity made him too nice to be tough. But knowing his life was in God's hands helped him accept whatever happened on the field and endure public criticism too.

Hard work and patience finally paid off in 1971. The Cowboys won the Super Bowl with a score of 24 to 3. Throughout the seventies, they stayed on top, went to five Super Bowls, and became so popular nationwide that they were called "America's Team."

The tide turned again in the eighties. Many of the best players had left the team or were getting too old. In 1984, Dallas missed the play-offs for the first time in ten years. In 1986, the Cowboys' twenty-year winning streak ended.

With many new, inexperienced players, the Cowboys lost thirteen games in 1988. Knowing the Cowboys would finally get a higher draft (get to pick players sooner), Tom looked forward to the challenge of rebuilding the team.

Sadly, he never got the chance. After the Cowboys were sold in 1989, the new owner rudely fired him. Reporters photographed the man celebrating with the new coach before Tom was even told he was being replaced. Tom accepted the blow with quiet dignity.

Following his firing, loyal fans showed their support. The Landrys received mountains of mail. Billboards were put up in Tom's honor. Tens of thousands of people lined the streets of Dallas on "Tom Landry Day."

Tom had led the Cowboys through twenty consecutive winning seasons, thirteen division championships, and five trips to the Super Bowl. He'd developed some of the best players in the business and changed forever the way football was played. But he will be most remembered as a national example of character and self-control.

D I S C U S S

Do you remember a time when your emotions or temper got the better of you? What were the results? What can you do to avoid "losing it" in the future?

48

JOHNNY CASH

IF YOU PUT AWAY THE SIN THAT IS IN YOUR HAND
AND ALLOW NO EVIL TO DWELL IN YOUR TENT, THEN
YOU WILL LIFT UP YOUR FACE WITHOUT SHAME; YOU
WILL STAND FIRM AND WITHOUT FEAR. (JOB 11:14–15)

Johnny Cash grew up during the Depression in a tiny, three-room house on a government-sponsored farm in Arkansas. His family was too poor to have electricity. But as he listened to a battery-powered radio by lantern light, he dreamed of becoming a star.

The Cash family was poor in material things, but they were rich in other ways. They had a loving Christian home. John's father was a deacon in the church. Even though they didn't own a car, the family rarely missed a service. They hitched rides in the back of a neighbor's truck until they got their first car when John was in high school.

He was especially close to his older brother, Jack, a devoted Christian. Jack's godly life inspired John and helped him decide to accept Christ himself at the age of twelve. In the years to come, he would find the stardom he'd dreamed of, but along the way he'd lose the peace he had known as a child.

He graduated from high school, joined the air force, and was stationed in Germany. When he came back, he married a girl named Vivian Liberto. Their happy home was soon blessed with children.

While working as a door-to-door salesman, he sang with a band that performed in churches. He also nagged the owner of a record company to give him an audition. The man finally listened and agreed to let him record two songs. In 1955, John was a guest on an Elvis Presley show, and his career took off. He began performing around the country and recorded two albums in 1958.

John and the musicians who worked with him often had to drive late at night to get to their next concert on time. One night one of them gave him a pill called a "bennie" to stay awake. The man assured him it was perfectly safe. After taking one, John was amazed at how refreshed and wide-awake he felt. Soon he was taking them regularly. Even though the constant traveling exhausted him, the pills pepped him up so that he could perform.

The pills were amphetamines, often used at the time by truck drivers to stay awake and by people who wanted to lose weight. For many years, John had no trouble getting prescriptions for them, because doctors didn't yet know they were dangerous.

The pills changed him. He developed twitches in his neck, back, and face. His nerves felt stretched to the point of breaking. He couldn't stand still, and he went days without sleeping. To calm down, he began to smoke heavily, drink a great deal, and take other drugs. This led to serious mood swings that frightened his wife and children. Vivian couldn't take the strain and filed for divorce.

His reckless driving destroyed countless cars. He became unpredictable and at times violent. During one performance, he became frustrated and threw a microphone stand, breaking fifty or sixty footlights. Concerts had to be canceled when he didn't show up. When he did, he often performed badly. He was jailed several times for public drunkenness.

With sheer willpower he got off the drugs a couple of times, but he couldn't stay drug free more than a week or two. The temptation was too strong. By this point doctors had realized how harmful amphetamines were, and he could no longer find doctors who would give them to him. He began to get them illegally. After being caught smuggling in drugs from Mexico, John was thrown in jail.

The sheriff was a fan of his. He made John realize that he'd die if he didn't get help. When John got home, he called June Carter, another country singer and a committed Christian. She called a doctor, who said he had never seen anyone overcome such a serious addiction.

John knew then that he couldn't kick the drug habit without God's help. June and her parents moved into his house to help him and pray with him through the nightmare of withdrawal. For three torturous weeks he felt much worse than he ever had on the drugs. His mind and body felt as if they would explode. He barely slept. But then things began to improve. After four weeks, friends who had thought he'd never make it began to believe he would.

After a time, John felt like a new person. He began going to church and doing concerts again. He tried to make up for problems he had caused. He repaid debts and did free concerts to make up for ones he had ruined. He also did prison concerts to tell of his faith and to show inmates that he cared about them. An album he did live at Folsom Prison sold more than five million copies. He rededicated his life to God and eventually asked June to marry him.

It wasn't all smooth sailing, though. He had one more slip on a visit to Vietnam during the war. The extreme heat, traveling, and exhausting schedule took their toll, and he became sick. Not wanting to disappoint the soldiers, he asked a doctor for antibiotics and some amphetamines in order to do the next shows.

The drugs made him worse, and he couldn't sleep. The next day he drank some brandy to clear his throat. The combination of drugs and alcohol left him in rough shape. Unable to finish a concert, John promised the soldiers they'd never see him in that condition again. The experience made him realize how much he needed to depend on God's help and how hard he had to work to resist temptation. He's stayed straight ever since.

Years later, he chose to recover from jaw surgery without painkillers rather than risk getting addicted to a medication. He later commented, "When you stand with [God], you must renew the stand daily; you must daily be on your guard. The hounds of hell are not going to stop snapping at your heels."[1]

John and June have witnessed to other entertainers. They've helped many overcome drug and alcohol problems. They've been frequent guests at Billy Graham crusades. John has written hundreds of gospel songs, and he and June produced a movie on the life of Jesus called *The Gospel Road,* which has brought hundreds to Christ.

DISCUSS

Few Christians are addicted to drugs and alcohol, but many struggle with some other sin they seem to repeat again and again. How can we apply what John learned to our own efforts to break sinful habits?

49
WILLIAM WILBERFORCE

LET US NOT BECOME WEARY IN DOING GOOD,
FOR AT THE PROPER TIME WE WILL REAP A
HARVEST IF WE DO NOT GIVE UP. (GALATIANS 6:9)

London was a dark place in the 1780s. Poor children worked as many as eighteen hours a day in cotton mills and coal mines, while many of their parents drank themselves into early graves. The rich gave little thought to the hungry and homeless crowding the city's streets. Instead, they spent their time drinking, gambling, having affairs, and counting their profits from the slave trade.

William Wilberforce, the son of a wealthy businessman, was too busy enjoying life to be bothered by the wrongs around him. He was a student at the University of Cambridge. He made several friends there who soon would become powerful men in Britain, including one who was elected the prime minister (like a president).

William was funny, charming, and popular. When he graduated, he ran for Parliament (Britain's body of lawmakers). Because of his well-known family, his speaking ability, and the generous feast he held for voters on election day, he won easily.

Members of both political parties liked him, and he was welcomed at all the best places and social events. He also went to church. But church going didn't really affect his actions until a pastor showed him that he needed to know Jesus personally. After he trusted in Christ and began reading his Bible, William saw how empty his lifestyle was. At first he wanted to get out of politics so that he could concentrate on God. A wise man told him to stay where he was and let God use him there.

When he tried to talk about his faith, though, his old friends thought he was crazy. They couldn't understand how such a well-educated man could get "carried away" with religion. But William wouldn't be quiet. He wrote a book, urging his countrymen to become saved and to live holy lives.

Then there was a revolution in France, and many powerful people in Britain began to feel uncertain about their own future. They read William's writings, became interested in spiritual things, and began attending church in large numbers.

At the same time, he found new friends who were committed to Christ. These Christian friends made him realize how horrible the slave trade was.

William Wilberforce then began what would become a long, bitter battle to pass a law so that no more slaves could be brought into Britain. The men who made money buying and selling slaves were very powerful and hard to fight. They bought votes in Parliament and argued that stopping the slave trade would hurt many other businesses in the country.

When William first asked for a law outlawing the evil practice, Parliament stalled. They agreed to gather information just so that they could put off making a decision. Year after year, William tried to get his law passed. He and his friends spent nine and ten hours a day reading and gathering evidence on the horrors and cruelty of slave trade. Finally, they went directly to the people and passed out thousands of pamphlets, spoke at public meetings, and persuaded them not to buy sugar that had been grown by slaves.

William's enemies struck back. They spread vicious lies about him and ridiculed him in political cartoons. Still he fought on. In 1796, with public opinion on his side, it looked as if his law would finally pass. But twelve of the men who supported it were so sure it would pass that they missed the final vote. It was defeated by four votes.

Every year he brought up his law in Parliament. War with France, his own illness, and political compromises kept it from passing. In 1804, one house of Parliament passed it; the other house didn't.

When the prime minister died, a man who was strongly against slavery took his place. By this time many English people thought slavery should be stopped. The new prime minister introduced William's law in one house of Parliament, and it passed. Then the law was brought up in the other house, and many members stood and praised William for working so long and hard to end the slave trade. As the house applauded him, he sat bent in his chair with tears running down his face. After a twenty-year struggle, the battle was finally won. Just days before he died, a law was passed that freed all slaves.

People throughout Britain had turned back to God. When William Wilberforce started his heroic fight, there were only two other committed Christians in Parliament. By the end of his life, there were more than one hundred in each house. God had used his and his friends' prayers and perseverance to change the heart of a nation.

DISCUSS

What are some wrongs in our society? Does stopping them seem impossible? What could you do to try?

50

DORIE VAN STONE

PRAISE BE TO THE GOD AND FATHER OF OUR LORD
JESUS CHRIST, THE FATHER OF COMPASSION AND THE
GOD OF ALL COMFORT, WHO COMFORTS US IN ALL
OUR TROUBLES, SO THAT WE CAN COMFORT THOSE
IN ANY TROUBLE WITH THE COMFORT WE OURSELVES
HAVE RECEIVED FROM GOD. (2 CORINTHIANS 1:3–4)

Dorie and her little sister, Marie, had no toys. They wore hand-me-down clothes that were badly worn and fit poorly. When their mother went to work, the girls were left alone in a drab, cold apartment. Before leaving, her mother always warned Dorie not to turn on any lights and to make sure that nothing happened to Marie.

While she was gone, Dorie made the only meal a six-year-old could fix: peanut butter and jelly sandwiches. Sometimes the two girls drank milk from jelly jar glasses, but usually they had only water. Their stomachs often growled with hunger.

But being poor wasn't the worst part of Dorie's life. What hurt far more was the way her mother acted toward her. She never hugged or kissed Dorie. If Dorie tried to get close to her, she pushed her away. She gave all her affection to Dorie's sister and often said, "Marie is a pretty girl—she's not like you."

Her father came to visit only a few times, but he liked Marie better, too. Dorie felt it was her fault that she was unwanted. She thought she must be very ugly. She kept her feelings to herself, though, because her mother spanked her whenever she cried.

Then one day her mother said she couldn't take care of the girls anymore and put both of them in an orphanage. Life there wasn't much better. Several of the women in charge of the children's home were mean. Dorie was whipped if she didn't eat all of her food, if she cried, or if she was caught reading when she was supposed to be working.

Once a month all the children were lined up so that people who were interested in adopting a child could look them over. Dorie was never chosen, and that made her feel even uglier.

After seven unhappy years in the orphanage, something happened that changed her life. A group of college students came one day and told the children a Bible story. The students also said that Jesus had died on the cross for them and that God loved them.

Somehow, Dorie knew it was true. That night she prayed silently, *They said You love me. Nobody else does. If You want me, You can have me!*[1] Instantly, she felt God beside her, and she had peace inside she had never had before.

A few weeks later, a nice woman came to work at the orphanage and took Dorie to church with her. On Dorie's thirteenth birthday, the woman gave her the first gift she had ever received—a New Testament.

Unfortunately, it wasn't long before Dorie and Marie had to leave, because the home kept children only up to the age of twelve. After that, they lived with an old woman and then with a family who knew their mother. Both treated Dorie cruelly. She was fed poorly and beaten repeatedly. Alone and afraid, she found her only comfort and hope in her Bible and in prayer.

At last, someone at school reported her bruises, and she was put in a home where she was not mistreated. During high school, she went to live with a doctor's family and worked as their maid. They saw some of her drawings, and they persuaded her to attend an art school.

Dorie got a good job drawing equipment for an aircraft company. Then she heard Darlene Diebler speak. Darlene was a former missionary to New Guinea. As Dorie listened, it seemed God wanted her to become a missionary to New Guinea, too. But she felt divided. She had been poor all of her life; she didn't want to give up her good job and the good things that came with it. But she decided to obey God, and she enrolled in a Bible school.

There she met another student, named Lloyd Van Stone. He fell in love with Dorie and asked her to marry him. Many people with a terrible past like hers are unable to love others, but God filled her heart with love for her husband and for the son and daughter who later blessed their home.

When they went to New Guinea as missionaries, she was also filled with love for the wild, uncivilized tribe they lived among. The Danis were cannibals. They never took baths from the time they were born until they died. They were filthy, smelly, and often pesky. But she loved them.

When their children got older, the mission society required that the children stay at a missionary school nearly two hundred miles away from their home. Their nine-year-old son became terrified that something would happen to his parents while he was away from them. When his fears wouldn't go away, Dorie and Lloyd decided to resign and return to North America.

Back in the United States, Dorie began speaking to church groups. She told others how God healed the crushed and bitter emotions of her past. Today she travels around the world with this message: "When no one else will love you, God will. He will always be there through thick and thin, good and bad. There is no comfort like His. He loves with a love that will never let you go."[2]

DISCUSS

How does Dorie's past make her message more convincing to people who have also been treated badly? What are some of the hardest things you've gone through? How could you use them to comfort others?

51

BILLY GRAHAM

A MAN'S PRIDE BRINGS HIM LOW, BUT A MAN OF
LOWLY SPIRIT GAINS HONOR. (PROVERBS 29:23)

He is one of the most respected and trusted men in the world. In the past forty years, the Gallup Poll has named him one of the Ten Most Admired Men thirty-three times. Many presidents and other world leaders have considered him a close friend. He has been called the greatest evangelist of all time. More than 200 million people have heard him speak. As a result, more than 3 million have trusted Christ.[1]

Even with this amazing record, Billy Graham remains a truly humble man. "I feel so undeserving of all the [Holy] Spirit has done," he has said, "because the work has been God's, not man's. I want no credit or glory. I want the Lord Jesus to have it all."[2]

Power and success have not changed him. Those who know him best say he believes what he preaches and lives what he believes. But while others praise his faithful and godly life, Billy says, "I share with [John] Wesley the feeling of my own inadequacy and sinfulness constantly. I am often amazed that God can use me at all."[3]

He refuses to take any credit for his preaching skill. Never claiming to be an intellectual, Billy preaches very simply. He has said that he only has one sermon with different versions. His message doesn't change, because the gospel doesn't change and human hearts don't change. He attributes his success to the power of prayer. Hundreds of prayer groups meet and pray for weeks before every crusade.

Another element of Billy's humble character is his willingness to put his own desires and comfort aside to obey God's plan. While he was growing up on a dairy farm in North Carolina, he dreamed of becoming a baseball player. He accepted Christ at the age of seventeen after hearing a traveling evangelist speak, and later he attended a Bible college in Florida. It was there that he began to sense that God was calling him to preach.

But his first try was a disaster. Even though he had four sermon outlines prepared, he became extremely nervous. With sweaty hands and shaking knees, he quickly went through his first sermon, then his second, and his third. After eight minutes he had gone through his fourth sermon and was very confused. With nothing left to say, he sat down. From then on he argued with the Lord, telling Him he *could* not preach, he did not *want* to preach, and he would not be *asked* to preach again.

Yet, the feeling that God wanted him to preach would not go away. He often prayed as he walked. Walking through a golf course late one night, he finally gave in, saying, "All right,

Lord, if You want me You've got me."[4]

For a while no one did ask him to preach. On top of being nervous, he had a thick Southern accent, and people thought he talked too loud and too fast and waved his arms too much. He prayed, and practiced privately. Then he began preaching on street corners and in front of bars. He was slugged by an angry barkeeper, thrown in a gutter by a gang, and often booed and laughed at. But he continued. Soon churches started asking him to come and preach.

After he became a minister, he went to Wheaton College in Illinois for more education. There he met a beautiful girl named Ruth, whom he later married. He became the pastor of a small church. Then another pastor asked him to take over a radio program in Chicago. He did, and the program became very popular.

The same man asked him to help him start an organization called Youth For Christ. Billy traveled for the next four years throughout America, Canada, and Europe, preaching to young people and starting local Youth For Christ groups.

In 1949, he held a series of meetings in Los Angeles in a huge tent. Each day more people came—so many that he stayed and preached there every day for eight weeks. The large crowds made news everywhere in the country, and Billy became famous. Soon he was traveling worldwide, preaching the gospel to bigger and bigger crowds.

This meant he was away from his wife and children for long periods of time. He missed them terribly and was often tempted to find a different career. But knowing God had called him to preach kept him going. He has kept on ever since, even when he has been harshly criticized and untrue things have been said about him.

In recent years the demands of his work and travel have become more difficult because of many health problems, including Parkinson's disease. As his physical strength grows weaker, Billy Graham leans on God's power more than ever and plans to preach as long as he possibly can.

DISCUSS

It's been said that humility is not thinking *less of ourselves* but, instead, thinking *of ourselves less*. What does this mean? List three or four ways Billy Graham did this. Describe a humble person you know. Think of some ways you could be more humble.

52

BOB WIELAND

HE REPLIED, "BECAUSE YOU HAVE SO LITTLE FAITH. I
TELL YOU THE TRUTH, IF YOU HAVE FAITH AS SMALL AS
A MUSTARD SEED, YOU CAN SAY TO THIS MOUNTAIN,
'MOVE FROM HERE TO THERE' AND IT WILL MOVE.
NOTHING WILL BE IMPOSSIBLE FOR YOU."

(MATTHEW 17:20–21)

As a high school and college student, Bob Wieland's goal was to become a professional baseball pitcher. He worked out with weights, played several other sports to stay in top shape, and practiced long and hard. After he pitched a game with nineteen strikeouts, scouts from the Phillies were nearly ready to sign him to a major league contract.

His dream seemed within reach until he received another offer he couldn't refuse—a draft notice requiring him to serve in the army. During army training, he was given the choice of becoming a medic or a cook. He chose to become a medic and was sent to Vietnam in 1969 at the height of the war.

He was in Vietnam only a few months when his unit, on patrol in the jungle, walked into a minefield. One of his best buddies was hit. As Bob rushed to help him, he stepped on a booby-trapped 82-millimeter mortar round—something that had enough explosive power to put a tank out of commission.

Doctors and nurses thought he was dead when he was brought into the hospital. The blast had taken off both legs, and he had lost nearly all of his blood. A doctor later told him he wouldn't have survived if he had gotten to the hospital fifteen seconds later.

During the next few days, the doctors still weren't sure he would live. On top of severe injuries, he had malaria. He was running a temperature of 105 to 106 degrees. He was given so much medicine for the pain and high fever that several days passed before he realized his legs were gone.

When he'd arrived in Vietnam, Bob was six feet tall, weighed two hundred five pounds, and looked like a professional weight lifter. Shortly after being wounded, he was two feet, ten and one-half inches tall and weighed eighty-seven pounds.

Although he grieved over the loss of his baseball career, Bob spent little time on self-pity. He had trusted Christ as a college sophomore, and now his faith brought him peace most people could not understand. He was deeply grateful to be alive, and he believed God had a special purpose for his life.

After long stays in different hospitals, he moved to California. He went back to college, got a degree in physical education, taught P. E., and met a special lady named Jackie, whom he eventually married.

He grew spiritually. He started speaking at high schools about striving for success. He also began weight lifting, pushing himself until he could lift more and more weight for longer times.

In time he competed in the bantamweight class in the United States Powerlifting Championships. At one hundred twenty-two pounds, he lifted three hundred three pounds—a new world record. But the judges refused to give him the title. Pointing to a rule book that said, "Contestants must be wearing shoes," they disqualified him. Later, he was banned from competition forever.

While he was wondering what God had in mind for him, Bob met an athletic trainer who asked him to try doing a lap around a track, walking on his hands and stumps. Although his hands were bruised and blistered when he finished, he made it around. After that, the trainer started working with him. Day after day he walked laps around the track, wearing small running shoes on his hands.

One day Bob told his trainer he wanted to walk across the United States on his hands and stumps to share his testimony and to raise money for the hungry. Believing nothing is impossible with God's help, he thought he could make the trip in a year. He trained hard for eighteen months. He worked out until he could do a pushup holding all of his weight on two fingers.

Then he set out. A friend came along to keep him company and drive a vehicle behind him. Along the way, Bob stopped to chat with people who came out to meet him, and he witnessed to many. Sometimes people they met invited them to stay in their homes; other times they spent the night in hotels or their vehicle. Bob also gave press conferences and speeches in different towns.

There were dangers and hardships. He walked in extreme heat in the desert and in temperatures as low as twenty-six degrees below zero in the winter. Drivers often couldn't see him at the side of the road because he was so low. Dogs were also a threat because he couldn't move quickly.

When he finally reached his goal—the Vietnam Memorial in Washington, D.C.—it had been three years, eight months, and six days since he'd left California. His walk raised more than $100,000 to feed the hungry, and many of the people Bob Wieland witnessed to came to know the Lord.

DISCUSS

Discuss the following: "God said faith can move mountains, but He didn't say we wouldn't need a shovel." Have you ever tried to do anything that seemed impossible? What happened? Is there anything you think God wants you to do that seems overwhelming?

53
ELISABETH ELLIOT

SURELY GOD IS MY SALVATION; I WILL TRUST AND
NOT BE AFRAID. THE LORD, THE LORD, IS MY
STRENGTH AND MY SONG; HE HAS BECOME MY
SALVATION. (ISAIAH 12:2)

Most people expected Elisabeth Elliot to take her young daughter, Valerie, and leave Ecuador when Auca Indians killed her husband. But she stayed on at Shandia, their mission station in the jungle. Although she missed Jim terribly, she went on working with the Quichua Indians.

But after a year, Elisabeth believed that God was moving her toward Auca work. Another missionary couple had come to Shandia, and the Quichua Christians were growing in their faith. In fact, the Quichuas were taking over much of their own preaching and teaching.

Her husband's murder had not made Elisabeth hate the Aucas. Instead, it had increased her desire to reach them. She once explained: "The fact that Jesus Christ died for all makes me interested in the salvation of all, but the fact that Jim loved and died for the Aucas intensifies [makes greater] my love for them."

That didn't mean she wasn't afraid or wasn't deeply concerned for Valerie's safety. Elisabeth prayed a great deal and believed that God would make clear what to do when the time was right. He did.

Elisabeth and Val were visiting another mission station when she heard that some Auca women had shown up at a nearby Quichua settlement. Certain that God wanted her to go and meet them, Elisabeth persuaded two reluctant Indians to guide her and Val on the six-hour walk through the jungle.

The sight of Elisabeth frightened the Aucas until they saw that she and the Quichuas were friends. The Quichuas in the settlement were also nervous. They believed other Aucas were planning an attack and had sent these two Auca women ahead as a distraction.

But when nothing happened over the next few days, the Quichuas began to relax and go back to their normal activities. The men went off on a hunt, and all of the women went to bathe in the river.

But the peace was suddenly broken by cries to get out of the river because Aucas were coming. They had already speared one man to death outside the village and had kidnapped his wife. With no men at home to defend them, the Quichua women believed they would all be killed. Elisabeth knew that was a real possibility.

The Aucas never actually came into the village, but the Quichuas moved away to be on the safe side. Elisabeth then took the two Auca women, Mintaka and Mankamu, back with her to Shandia.

Once they were settled, Elisabeth began working very hard to learn the Auca language. Even though the women did not understand Quichua or English, they believed everyone understood *their* language. They talked at full speed and became offended when Elisabeth didn't know what they said—until they finally realized that she really couldn't understand them.

In the meantime, Rachel Saint (the sister of one of the other murdered missionaries) was in the United States. With her was Dayuma, an Auca woman who'd left the tribe years ago and had become a Christian. Rachel sent Elisabeth what information she had learned about the language from Dayuma. As Elisabeth learned to speak in Auca, she started teaching Mintaka and Mankamu about God and what the Bible said.

When nearly a year had passed, Mankamu told Elisabeth she wanted to go back to her family and take Elisabeth and her little girl with her. Elisabeth asked if it would be safe. Mankamu said she and Mintaka would tell their people that Elisabeth was good and was their friend. They would also tell their people what God's Word said and that they should believe in God. By this time, Rachel and Dayuma were back in Ecuador, and Dayuma went with Mankamu and Mintaka to tell the Aucas about the kind white women.

While waiting for their return, Elisabeth had many mixed emotions. She didn't want to leave her Quichua friends, whom she understood and loved. It was also hard to leave her cozy home with its walls, floors, and furniture—things she'd have to live without among the Aucas. She wondered whether she should leave Val behind. After much prayer, she decided that God wanted her to trust Him for the safety of both of them.

Then the three Auca women returned, along with seven more Aucas. They assured Elisabeth that their people would welcome her. On October 6, 1958, Elisabeth, Val, and Rachel set out for the jungle with the Aucas. Some Quichua men went along to help carry their belongings.

The group traveled by canoe and on foot for several days until they arrived at the Auca village. The men and women were naked except for a cotton string around their hips. Some of them had great holes in their earlobes, which they had plugged with large chunks of balsa wood. The women had shaved or plucked all of their eyebrows.

The Aucas built a house for Elisabeth and Valerie exactly like the houses they lived in. It had a roof made of leaves and had no walls or floor. The only furniture was a small table, the bamboo slab Val slept on, and a hammock, which Elisabeth slept in at night and sat on during the day.

Every day Elisabeth and Rachel made careful notes on the Auca language—it had never been written down—so that one day the Bible could be translated into Auca. There was little protection from rain, and Elisabeth kept her language papers in plastic bags or hung them high enough under the roof that they wouldn't get wet.

Like the Aucas, she kept a fire going for cooking, to keep insects and animals away, and to provide warmth at night. The fire wasn't foolproof; one night she found a snake coiled near Val's head as she slept.

For food, the Aucas grew manioc (a root) and plantain (an herb). They also ate fish, monkey, squirrel, toucan, macaw, wild hog, and grubs (the larvae of a giant beetle). Elisabeth and Val ate Indian food when it was offered, but they also had food dropped to them by parachute. In turn, they shared that with the Aucas.

After two years, Elisabeth believed it was time to go back to the United States so that Valerie, who was then six, could learn from and with other students. Rachel remained with the Aucas and was eventually joined by other missionaries and translators. In 1992, the Auca Indians received the New Testament in their own language.

DISCUSS

It's been said that the better we know God, the easier it becomes to trust Him. The more we trust Him, the easier it becomes to obey Him. The more we obey Him, the more we see how trustworthy He is. In what ways did Elisabeth's life prove all this to be true? In what ways does yours?

54

BILL BRIGHT

DO YOU NOT SAY, "FOUR MONTHS MORE AND THEN
THE HARVEST"? I TELL YOU, OPEN YOUR EYES AND
LOOK AT THE FIELDS! THEY ARE RIPE FOR HARVEST.

(JOHN 4:35)

Bill Bright had one goal: to make lots of money. And he seemed likely to succeed. As a college student in Oklahoma, he displayed leadership and ambition. He was president of his student body. He was listed in *Who's Who in American Colleges and Universities*.

After graduating, he moved to Los Angeles and started a business selling fancy foods throughout the United States and Canada. With his hard work and long hours, the business prospered.

Although his mother was a godly woman, Bill was an agnostic (someone who thinks it's impossible to know if there is a God). But his mother's prayers started to catch up with him one day. He picked up a hitchhiker who invited Bill to come home with him. The hitchhiker was living with Dawson Trotman, and Dawson Trotman was the man who had started The Navigators, an organization that teaches Christians to witness to others. In spite of himself, Bill was impressed with Dawson's loving attitude.

About the same time, the elderly couple Bill lived with kept urging him to come to their church. He finally went and was then invited to a party for the church's young adults. The happy group attracted him. He began to attend church regularly and joined a Sunday school class taught by Henrietta Mears. In a short time he gave his heart to the Lord.

Never one to do anything halfway, he hired someone to manage his business while he went to Princeton Seminary in New Jersey to learn more about his new faith. His business suffered, though, so he moved back to California where he could both take care of business and attend the new Fuller Seminary.

By this time he was falling for a pretty girl from his hometown. There was one big problem, however. Vonette Zachary wasn't a Christian, and she thought he was a fanatic. All that changed when Henrietta Mears led Vonette to the Lord. Bill and Vonette married in 1948.

The newlyweds made a list of what they wanted in life. But as they looked at their list, they realized that many of their desires were for worldly gain and comfort. They wrote new goals, which included things such as living holy lives and being effective witnesses for Christ. As a lasting reminder, they drew up a written contract with the Lord, surrendering their lives to Him.

After they did this, God gave Bill an idea of what his life's work would be: to present the gospel to as many people in the world as he could, starting with college students. He was so eager to get started that he dropped out of seminary and sold his business. He and Vonette moved into a rented house a block from the University of California at Los Angeles.

Living on money from his business, they started having meetings for students in their home. In a few months' time more than two hundred fifty UCLA students had given their lives to Christ. They named their tiny ministry Campus Crusade for Christ.

Soon Christians at other campuses were asking the Brights to bring Campus Crusade to their schools. Bill and Vonette worked out of several different locations and hired six men to help them. The ministry grew fast. In 1960 there were 109 staff members working on forty campuses in fifty states, and work was started in South Korea, Pakistan, and Mexico.

Because of this rapid growth, Bill saw the need for a tool for sharing the gospel, and he wrote a small booklet called *The Four Spiritual Laws*. In a simple way, the booklet talked about God's love, man's sinfulness, the person and work of Christ, and the need of each person to make a decision to follow Jesus. It proved to be a highly effective witnessing tool and has introduced tens of millions around the world to the gospel ever since.

The businessman in Bill Bright has continually looked for new and better ways to "sell" Christianity. The Crusade has expanded to work in high schools, inner cities, and prisons and to reach laymen, government leaders, and executives. Special teams have used sports, music, drama, and the media to present the gospel.

Campus Crusade brought together high school and college students from a thousand cities at Explo '72 in order to learn about Christ and how to witness for Him. One hundred eighty thousand gathered the last day to hear Christian rock groups, Johnny Cash and June Carter, and Billy Graham. Two years later, Explo '74 was held in South Korea, with more than three hundred thousand delegates attending. Two evening rallies drew more than 1.3 million people.

In 1976, the "I Found It" campaign was carried out in 246 cities. Billboards and bumper stickers generated interest with the words "I Found It!" More than three hundred thousand Christians were trained by Campus Crusade to explain what they had found—new life in Jesus.

In 1979, Campus Crusade produced a film on the life of Jesus. The *Jesus* movie has since been translated into 400 languages. One of the most effective missionary tools ever developed, it has been seen by 850 million people.[1]

Today, Campus Crusade has more than forty different ministries with full-time staff and trained volunteers in more than one hundred sixty-seven countries. Ever one to believe in the possibility of the impossible with God's help, Bill Bright keeps dreaming bigger and bigger dreams.

Working under a plan called New Life 2000, his goal is to see Campus Crusade, along with other ministries, reach the world's six billion people with the gospel by the year 2000. Using the *Jesus* film, translated radio broadcasts of it, and ministry teams, he hopes to reach even the most obscure corners of the planet. He explains, "We've taken the *Jesus* film into places where they've never seen a white man, or a movie of any kind."[2]

The Crusade is also building a World Center for Discipleship and Evangelism in Orlando, Florida. Its 285-acre campus will include a retreat center and a training/conference center.

In 1995, Campus Crusade was ranked as the "biggest" religious charity, outranking Focus on the Family and the Billy Graham Evangelistic Association. In 1996, it took in nearly $300 million worldwide. If Bill Bright were the head of a business that brought in that much money, he would probably receive a huge salary. Instead, he earns a modest $29,000 a year.[3] Years ago, he realized he'd find more joy in saving souls than in making money.

DISCUSS

Do you hesitate to witness because you think most people don't want to hear "anything religious"? How does this attitude contradict (disagree with) the verse in John? Compare this attitude with Bill Bright's outlook.

55

KENNETH N. TAYLOR

LET THE WORD OF CHRIST DWELL IN YOU RICHLY
AS YOU TEACH AND ADMONISH ONE ANOTHER WITH
ALL WISDOM, AND AS YOU SING PSALMS, HYMNS, AND
SPIRITUAL SONGS WITH GRATITUDE IN YOUR
HEARTS TO GOD. (COLOSSIANS 3:16)

Ken Taylor often felt guilty because he didn't enjoy reading his Bible more. He grew up in Oregon in the 1920s. He came from a strong Christian family, he received Christ at an early age, and he knew that regular Bible study was important. His father often told him and his brother, Doug, "Unless you fellows get into the Word of God and get the Word of God into your lives, you'll never amount to much as Christians."[1]

But Ken struggled to understand the King James Bible, which his family and most Christians used at that time. It was written in English as it was spoken in the seventeenth century. Many words were very different from twentieth-century English.

Ken did his best to live the way a Christian should, though. During his high school years, he enjoyed track and debate, often earned straight A's, joined a Bible study group, and met a girl named Margaret, whom he would later marry. Like many young people who lived through the Great Depression, he dreamed of becoming rich and famous. He planned to accomplish this by becoming a doctor.

It was while he was a student at Wheaton College that Ken read a book about another college student named Bill Borden. That book changed his goal. Bill Borden had an incredible love for God and other people. His wealthy father left him a million dollars, and he gave away hundreds of thousands. Borden had planned to become a missionary to the Muslim world, but he died on the way.

The young man's devotion deeply touched Ken. Becoming rich no longer seemed important. When he finished the book, he got on his knees and asked the Lord to take his life and use it any way He wanted to. In his senior year at Wheaton, he took an aptitude test that showed he would not do well as a doctor.

After graduation, he worked with InterVarsity Christian Fellowship in Canada, traveling and speaking at different schools. He still had difficulty with the King James Bible. He recalls being asked to speak on a chapter in Ephesians that totally baffled him. As he tried to study it, he became so frustrated that he exclaimed, "Why can't somebody translate the Bible so a person like me can understand it?"[2]

He went to seminary in Dallas and married Margaret. Once he finished his training, he became the editor of InterVarsity's new magazine called *HIS*, and he moved Margaret and his first child to Chicago.

Hoping to reach more non-Christians, he joined Good News Publishers, which published tracts (leaflets about salvation) used overseas. Later, he directed Moody Literature Mission, where he developed Christian books for poor countries. For thirteen years, he directed both Moody Literature Mission and Moody Press.

Christian publishers were having a hard time selling books just then. Many of their books lost money. To change this, Ken started the Christian Booksellers Association, which helped Christian publishers and bookstores succeed.

His publishing work was highly rewarding, emotionally if not financially. Raising their large family (ten children in all) left little money to spare. He and Margaret were married seven years before they bought their first car, and it was twenty years old. Because World War Two caused a serious housing shortage in Chicago, they had a hard time finding a home they could afford. They finally bought an old two-story farmhouse that had no cupboards in the kitchen and no heat in the children's bedrooms.

For many years they couldn't afford a television. Even after they could, Ken chose not to buy one because of TV's negative influence. Instead, he led his family in devotions every night after dinner.

He couldn't find a Bible storybook for very young children that covered the entire Bible, so he decided to write one himself. The result was *The Bible in Pictures for Little Eyes,* which has been published in more than sixty languages and has sold more than a million copies.

Ken also wrote some devotional books, but he wanted to read the actual Bible to his older children. When he tried to read his King James Bible to them, he couldn't hold their attention. Their reaction reminded him of the frustration he'd felt himself in his younger days. He prayed about the problem and came up with the idea to rewrite each verse to make it more understandable. After he finished a chapter, he tried it on his kids. They understood it all and were much more interested.

He came to believe that God wanted him to reword all of the letters in the New Testament in order to help other families. But where would he find the time? With his job and growing family, he had little to spare. He decided to write while he rode the commuter train to and from work. Then each night, after the children were in bed, he checked what he'd done with commentaries and Greek word studies.

He worked for seven years, revising his work six times. He finished *Living Letters* in 1960. To his surprise, he couldn't find a publisher who was willing to print it. Believing there was a great need for it, though, Ken decided to publish the book himself. He had 2,000 copies printed.

He sold 867 copies at the Christian Booksellers' Convention, but four months went by and there were no new orders. He wondered how he'd get rid of the rest of the books. Then things picked up just before the Christmas season. Within a year, 75,000 copies had been sold.

Although he had only one product to publish, Ken named his company Tyndale House Publishers after the man who had been killed for translating the Bible into English.

Then one day he was told that Billy Graham wanted to give a copy of *Living Letters* to anyone who asked for it after seeing Billy on television. Billy asked how much payment per book he would need. Ken said none. Billy insisted that he get something, so they agreed on 5¢ a copy. Billy's organization had 600,000 copies printed.

When the $30,000 check came, Ken didn't even think of using it for himself, even though his family was living in an old, crowded farmhouse in great need of repair. Instead, he started the Tyndale Foundation, which would eventually give millions of dollars to Christian work around the world.

Then he began to feel he should quit the job he loved and spend all of his time paraphrasing the rest of the Bible. With ten children to feed and limited finances, this took a great deal of faith.

He finished *The Living Bible* in 1971 and published the first edition on credit. In 1972 and 1973, it was the fastest selling book in America and quickly zoomed into millions of sold copies. More than 36 million copies have now been sold.

Much of the profit has been used to translate the Bible into other languages through Living Bibles International. More than fifty New Testament translations have been completed and fifteen translations of the whole Bible.

Tyndale House, which began with one book, has published many other best-selling Christian books as well.

DISCUSS

Do you enjoy reading the Bible? Considering what Ken Taylor did, what could you do to make your Bible study more enjoyable?

56

CLEBE AND DEANNA McCLARY

MANY A MAN CLAIMS TO HAVE UNFAILING LOVE, BUT
A FAITHFUL MAN WHO CAN FIND? (PROVERBS 20:6)

Clebe McClary lettered in high school football, basketball, and track. He won the state championship in the mile. He went to college with the help of an athletic scholarship and became a high school coach. When he started teaching, several female high school students developed crushes on the tall, dark, handsome teacher—including a beautiful blonde cheerleader named Deanna.

In Deanna's case it was more than a passing crush. They were married in 1967. Their honeymoon was only a few days long because Clebe was on a short leave from Marine Corps training. A deeply patriotic man, he had joined the Marines so that he could serve his country during the Vietnam War. He had just passed Officer Candidate School and become a second lieutenant.

In Vietnam, he volunteered for reconnaissance duty. That meant he'd lead a platoon scouting behind enemy lines. Deanna thought it sounded like a suicide mission, but he knew he would be good at such work. He had grown up hunting and had learned how to move quietly and to stop and listen carefully.

He wrote Deanna letters, then started to send his messages on cassette tapes. On one tape he interrupted his letter shouting, "Gotta go! Incoming." In his hurry he left the tape running. As Deanna later listened to the tape, she heard the enemy bombs in the background and fast-forwarded to see if he came back!

Throughout his first five months, Clebe didn't lose one of his men—an unusual record for a recon crew. Although he wasn't a Christian at the time, he believed that God had protected him and his troops many times. He only had one patrol to go before he would be released for a brief rest and to see Deanna.

On that last patrol, Clebe and his twelve men went into an area where few men had been. They were dropped by helicopter onto a hill near a small tea plantation. His men quickly dug foxholes and took cover in a pit and bomb crater and waited. The enemy fired on them off and on for two days. Finally the operation was canceled. But bad weather kept the helicopters from coming to pick them up.

The third night was quiet until midnight. Then, thinking he heard enemy movement, Clebe grabbed his weapon. Before he could organize his men, a grenade landed in the pit.

Shrapnel (pieces of metal) hit his face, neck, and shoulder. He yelled to his radioman to call for air support.

In an instant a squad of North Vietnamese soldiers ran up the hill. They were on a suicide mission and had explosives strapped to their bodies. One jumped in front of Clebe. Clebe shot him, but he fell into the pit and his grenades exploded. Clebe was thrown into the air by the blast, and his left arm was torn off below the elbow.

Many of his men were unconscious or dead. Clebe fought on, knowing they would all be killed otherwise. He darted from one spot to another, directing his men until another grenade took his legs out from under him. He lay very still, pretending to be dead. An enemy soldier shot him, but the bullet passed through his neck. A few minutes later, a buddy dragged him into a helicopter that had gotten there just in time.

Back home, Deanna was looking forward to her reunion with her husband. Instead, a Marine officer and a doctor came to her door with the news of what had happened. They said he had lost his left arm and been badly wounded. She was also told his chances of surviving were slim.

Clebe did survive, but it was two months before he was stable enough to be moved to a hospital in the States. He wondered what Deanna's reaction would be. Every day, he knew, wives came who turned and walked away from badly injured husbands. He couldn't help wondering if his young, beautiful wife would be better off without a mangled husband to care for.

When Deanna arrived at the hospital, she thought she heard Clebe's voice and peeked around a door. She saw a man with a bandaged head, one eye, huge red scars, jagged stitches, broken teeth, and swollen lips. She didn't think the man was Clebe, though, because it looked as if he had no arms. Actually, his right arm was in a cast, bound against his body. As soon as she heard his voice again, she knew it was her husband, and she rushed to his side. She told him how much she loved him and promised that they would always be together.

On his first leave from the hospital, Clebe and Deanna went to an evangelistic crusade where both of them gave their hearts to the Lord. God's strength in their lives helped them make it through years of rehabilitation.

He had more than twenty operations. But both of his legs were saved, and at last he regained some use of his right hand. As Deanna helped with his daily therapy, she saw beyond the scabs, scars, stitches, and metal sticking out of his body. She was inspired by his strength and determination and loved him even more.

Deanna and Clebe opened a coffeehouse to show young people the way to Jesus. Later, Clebe wrote a book about his experiences, and they traveled about the country telling what the Lord had done for them.

DISCUSS

Think of a friend or loved one who went through a very difficult time. Did you help him? In what way? Are there things you didn't do or say that you wish you had?

57

ROMULO SAUNE

I AM TORN BETWEEN THE TWO: I DESIRE TO DEPART
AND BE WITH CHRIST, WHICH IS BETTER BY FAR;
BUT IT IS MORE NECESSARY FOR YOU THAT I
REMAIN IN THE BODY. (PHILIPPIANS 1:23–24)

High in the mountains of Peru, a small boy in a tattered shirt, patched pants, and bare feet watched his sheep. Although poor in material things, Romulo Saune was rich in other ways. His mother's father, Justiniano Quicana, was a direct descendant of Inca royalty. Justiniano gave him a deep sense of pride in his background. Romulo also inherited great spiritual wealth. After his grandfather accepted Christ, the whole Quicana family became believers.

Romulo's father, however, wanted his mother to go back to their people's old ways and religion. When she refused, he left. Romulo and his mother went to live with her godly parents, but she never stopped praying for her husband.

His mother's family had been the first believers in their village. They led others to the Lord. Then Justiniano and his oldest son started churches. Other relatives became pastors, teachers, and evangelists. People who opposed the gospel threatened to burn down the Quicanas' house. They told Romulo's mother that they would kill her children "like frogs." But they trusted God to protect them.

Romulo was a happy child even though he did have a difficult time in school because of a freak accident. In his village, children sometimes raced one another, riding on the backs of pigs. One day Romulo's pig ran toward some horses, and he was kicked in the head. He lost his hearing in one ear and developed learning disabilities. To make things even harder, his teacher spoke only Spanish and didn't understand the Quechua language that Romulo spoke. For many years he had to work very hard until he caught up to his classmates.

After a while his father became a Christian and a traveling evangelist. This meant he was still gone most of the time. Romulo's mother took her children and her youngest brother, who was only a year older than Romulo, and moved to the closest large city, so that the boys could get a better education.

In the city, the boys saw cars and paved roads for the first time. The family struggled to get by. The Spanish people looked down on the Indians and treated them rudely. Romulo worked as a servant for a Spanish family, even though he couldn't understand Spanish. He also sold newspapers, shined shoes, and later worked in a bakery. There were daily terrorist attacks by a revolutionary Communist group called The Shining Path, which wanted to take over

Peru.

By the time he was in high school, not only was he at the top of his class, but he also was learning English and had become a language helper for Wycliffe missionaries. They were making a simpler translation of the New Testament using the Quechua language.

Romulo injected fun into everything he did. When he taught young boys in his church, he added lively music to the lessons. When he played different characters on Bible tapes, he did so with dramatic flair. He was a popular Christian speaker, and his laughter and friendliness delighted audiences.

Donna, the daughter of Wycliffe missionaries, couldn't resist his charm or loving spirit. They married while he was studying in California at the Latin America Bible Institute.

Romulo and Donna returned to Peru to find things worse than before. The Shining Path was gaining power. It had become one of the most violent terrorist groups in the world. The Shining Path members killed or frightened anyone who stood in their way. These revolutionists especially hated Christians because Christians wouldn't join their group.

In spite of the dangers, Romulo and the Quicana family continued to lead the Quechua Christians. They started an independent mission called TAWA. Justiniano welcomed weary travelers to his home, preached the Word, and gave them Christian literature.

Because he influenced many people, The Shining Path burned down Justiniano's house and kidnapped his wife. They tortured and beat her, and she survived only because they thought she was dead.

But Romulo knew many members of The Shining Path from high school days, and he led several to Christ. He wrote Quechan-style Christian songs, helped organize a crusade, trained outreach teams, and helped revise the first draft of a Quechan Old Testament. Starting every day with prayer, he always expected the best and dreamed of turning his city to Christ.

Because he cared about everyone, he was well loved. The Shining Path noticed his popularity and started threatening him. One day they surrounded his house and fired machine guns. His son, who was home alone, hid in the attic and wasn't harmed.

Realizing his family wasn't safe, he decided to move to Lima. On the way, he saw a terrorist roadblock ahead. He turned their Jeep off the road, and they careened down the hillside, barely missing trees and boulders. They narrowly escaped.

Further down the highway, a large truck slammed into their Jeep and began pushing it toward the edge of a cliff. Romulo's mother prayed, then commanded the truck to stop in the name of Jesus. Instantly the truck stopped. The family finally arrived in the city safely.

When word got out that Romulo was in Lima, pastors started coming at all hours to talk with him. They came with heavy hearts for their hurting people. He became a pastor's pastor, offering advice, comfort, and friendship.

One day he received news that his grandfather had been tortured and stabbed to death by the terrorists. Friends urged him to leave Peru before he too was killed, but he wouldn't turn his back on his countrymen. Many times he longed for the peace and joy of heaven, but he hoped he'd be spared for a time to reach more Quechuas.

The TAWA mission grew, and Romulo became president. By this time he was speaking in different places around the world to draw attention to his people's troubles.

In 1992, he returned from a huge conference, loaded down with gifts for friends and relatives. He took them with him when he went to a festival in the village where he grew up. His family had to sleep in caves and other hiding places because of the danger, but he was thrilled to be back. He wanted to bring some happiness to people who had suffered so much. He did his best to see that everyone had a good time and made sure they all had plenty to eat.

After he had preached about the glories of heaven, he passed out his gifts and cookies and candy to all the children. Knowing it was only a matter of time before The Shining Path killed him, he told his friends he'd see them in heaven if he didn't see them again on earth.

On the way home, Romulo's vehicle was stopped by a terrorist roadblock. He and several family members were gunned down. One week after their deaths, the leader of the revolutionists was caught, and within a few months nearly twenty-five hundred terrorists had been captured.

Romulo is in heaven, but his ministry lives on through TAWA, the Scriptures he helped translate, the songs he wrote, and the lives he touched.

D I S C U S S

Has there been a time in your life when heaven seemed especially real to you? Why? How can thinking about heaven affect our outlook on life today?

58

HAROLD MORRIS

BE VERY CAREFUL, THEN, HOW YOU LIVE—NOT AS
UNWISE BUT AS WISE, MAKING THE MOST OF EVERY
OPPORTUNITY, BECAUSE THE DAYS ARE EVIL.

(EPHESIANS 5:15–16)

Harold Morris was a star athlete in Georgetown, South Carolina. He was captain of his high school football, basketball, and baseball teams. He received many college scholarship offers. Unfortunately, he didn't do as well in the classroom. He was too busy drinking beer and chasing girls. His poor grades made him ineligible to get into most colleges, let alone participate in sports.

Harold graduated, got a job, married the high school beauty queen, and moved to North Carolina. But he wasn't ready to settle down. He ignored his wife's wishes and went on drinking and running around with his buddies. In time, his wife had enough of this kind of behavior.

After their divorce, Harold began spending time with characters he met in nightclubs. He started to use drugs. And his choice of friends led to terrible consequences that changed his entire life.

In September of 1968, he and two other men went to Atlanta to hit the nightclubs. On their way out of town, they made a stop. Harold waited in the car while his friends went into a grocery store. The men came back, running and shouting, "Drive! Drive! We shot a man!" Dazed and panic-stricken, he did as they commanded. His friends assured him the man's wound was not serious.

Months later, his so-called friends were caught. They blamed him for the murder and other crimes they'd committed. He was tried and convicted for armed robbery and murder. He was given two life sentences for crimes he didn't do.

Harold spent two and one-half years in a county jail and then became convict #62345 in the Georgia State Penitentiary. Known as one of the worst prisons in the country, it was crowded and filthy and crawling with roaches, ants, and flies. There was no privacy. The most violent prisoners controlled the other prisoners. At times, riots broke out between blacks and whites.

He saw dozens of murders and stabbings. He was wounded himself and had his life threatened many times. On the outside he acted tough, so that the other inmates wouldn't know how terrified he was. There was no one he could trust, and he was terribly lonely. His family didn't even know he was in prison, and he refused to let them know.

One night, just in time, Harold saw an inmate swing a board toward his head. A split-second move to the side saved his life, but the board still smashed the side of his skull. In self-defense, he grabbed the man and began choking him. With blood gushing from his head and a cut on his arm, he was afraid he would bleed to death before the guards came. It took thirty-nine stitches to close up his wound.

But Harold was blamed for the fight and was illegally sentenced to death row for as long as he remained in the prison. He spent every day by himself in a small cell. The only time he could leave was to shower once a week. He'd survived five years in prison, but the hopelessness of being on death row the rest of his life overwhelmed him. He thought about committing suicide.

For as long as he could remember, Harold had refused to believe in God. Now in desperation he cried out, "God, if You are real, take my life or free me!"[1] Two weeks later he was moved to the "trusty" building—the best place in the prison! But he didn't give God the credit for the change.

Shortly after the move, his brother and mother came to visit. They had finally found out where he was. Just knowing that they still loved him in spite of the mess he had made of his life gave him hope. His brother asked Clebe McClary to visit him. Clebe had played football and basketball with Harold in high school. After being badly wounded in Vietnam, he had become a Christian.

Clebe and his wife visited him and left a tape of Clebe's testimony and a list of Bible verses. As Harold listened to the tape and read the verses, he realized how badly he needed Christ. With tears streaming down his face, he begged Jesus to forgive him and come into his heart.

From then on, he prayed for his release, promising God he would serve Him when he was free. But one day he realized that God wanted him to serve Him wherever he was, and he began reaching out and witnessing to other inmates. This took a great deal of courage, since many prisoners considered Christians weak and tried to provoke them into fights.

Harold became such a model prisoner that he was asked to speak in high schools about the dangers of alcohol and drugs. Soon he was receiving letters from hundreds of teenagers, asking him for advice. He answered every letter and helped many young people.

In 1978, he was released on parole and went to work in a home for troubled boys—coaching, counseling, and loving them. He also began going back to the penitentiary to speak and visit inmates. Many became Christians through his witness, including some of the most dangerous criminals in the prison.

Later, Harold went to a Bible college and began giving his testimony at churches. Three years after he was paroled, he was given a full pardon. This allowed him to travel freely and speak at prisons, schools, and churches throughout the United States. He also witnessed nationwide through radio and television and personally discipled many of the prisoners he led to Christ.

In 1984, Harold learned he had cancer behind his left ear, in his sinuses, tongue, throat, and lymph nodes. His doctor told him he might live three years with treatment and gave him maximum doses of radiation, which left him in physical misery. When the cancer was finally gone, another crisis developed. His throat now was so full of scar tissue that it was almost completely closed. The doctor said he'd have to remove Harold's vocal cords and insert an eating tube. He would never be able to talk or eat normally again.

Because Harold didn't want to stop telling others about Christ, he said no. The doctor told him the only other choice was to learn to push a two-and-a-half-foot rubber rod down his throat every day. The first experience took him half a day and left blood, vomit, and tears all over the bathroom. But he kept on until he mastered the process, and then he was out speaking again.

He raised money for Christmas gifts for prisoners and included with each gift a copy of a book he'd written about his life. Many prisoners had tears in their eyes when they received the gifts. Others wrote thank-you letters telling him how the Lord used his book in their lives.

Today Harold no longer speaks publicly. Doing so tires him too much, but he is working at home on another book and a film about his life. Harold Morris still wants to help others.

DISCUSS

Do you know someone God has used in an unlikely situation? Discuss the following quote: "Opportunities come dressed in overalls more often than tuxedos."

59
FLORENCE NIGHTINGALE

WHAT IS MORE, I CONSIDER EVERYTHING A LOSS
COMPARED TO THE SURPASSING GREATNESS OF
KNOWING CHRIST JESUS MY LORD, FOR WHOSE SAKE
I HAVE LOST ALL THINGS. I CONSIDER THEM RUBBISH,
THAT I MAY GAIN CHRIST. (PHILIPPIANS 3:8)

Florence Nightingale had everything a child in nineteenth-century England could dream of. Her parents were extremely wealthy. They had servants. They had two large homes. Their winter house had a ballroom; their summer house had fifteen bedrooms. The family took long, expensive vacations. They went to fancy parties, operas, and balls with other "high society" (rich) people.

Florence had an excellent mind too. Her father taught her Greek, Latin, German, French, Italian, history, and philosophy. He also taught her to read the Bible from the Greek text. Her mother thought it unnecessary for a girl to spend so much time studying. She expected Florence to marry a rich young man and go on living in luxury.

As Florence grew older, though, she became more and more uneasy about her lifestyle. In the 1840s, England went through an economic depression. Most of the common people were very poor. Many were actually starving. She couldn't enjoy all she had, while knowing so many were living in misery.

Her life felt empty until she had a special experience when she was sixteen. Alone in her room one day, she was sure God was telling her to serve Him in a special way. She felt content, knowing He would show her what she was to do when the time was right. In the meantime, she studied math for hours. Years later, her mathematical abilities would be very helpful in the work she was called to.

She also began taking medicine, food, and clothes to the cottages of the poor and caring for them when they were sick. By the time she was twenty-four, she was sure of what God wanted her to do—work in hospitals among the sick. Her family was horrified and flatly refused. Her mother was ashamed that she wanted to do something so "degrading."

But Florence was unwilling to give up her desire to help the sick. She refused two marriage proposals, even though she loved one of the suitors. Her mother and sister became so angry they would hardly speak to her.

In 1844, hospitals were dark, poorly run, and disgusting. Floors were never scrubbed, and walls were covered with dirt and mold. Many times patients came in filthy and stayed that way. People with all kinds of different diseases were crammed into the same room. The smell was often so bad that doctors made their rounds holding handkerchiefs over their noses. Because respectable women wouldn't work in hospitals, nurses were often drunken, careless, and dirty themselves.

Florence read government reports on hospital care in Great Britain and on the continent. Torn between what she felt God had called her to do and pleasing her family, she had a nervous breakdown when she was twenty-seven.

Friends sent her to Rome for a rest. While there, she met Sidney Herbert, a friend who would later help her in her work. She also visited a hospital in Germany where caring churchwomen nursed the sick. Seeing the difference that good nursing could make gave Florence the courage to finally pursue her dream.

She heard about a well-run hospital in Paris, operated by nuns, and she went there to learn all she could. She visited many other hospitals. She sent out questionnaires to hospitals in France, Germany, and England.

Her years of study and research made her an expert in nursing care. When she was thirty-three, she was put in charge of a London charity hospital. It was exhausting work from dawn until nightfall, but she loved it. Then she left in 1854 to direct nurses battling an outbreak of cholera (an infectious intestinal disease that is usually fatal) sweeping through the London slums.

At the same time, events were taking place a continent away that would change Florence's life. Turkey, Britain, and France declared war on Russia after Russia attacked Turkey's ships. During the war that followed, an epidemic (widespread illness) of cholera broke out. British newspapers reported that thousands of sick and wounded soldiers were suffering and dying because of poor care.

Nurses had never been allowed to work in army hospitals, but now the government called for volunteers. Sidney Herbert, Florence's old friend, had become Britain's secretary at war. He asked her to go to Turkey and manage the hospital at the military base there. Before she left, she bought supplies with her own money.

What Florence and the other nurses saw when they arrived shocked them. Four miles of wounded soldiers lay a foot or so apart in old, rundown, filthy barracks. This makeshift hospital had no kitchen, no running water, no supplies, and little food. It was crawling with rats and bugs.

The doctors didn't like a woman's trying to change things, and they ignored her. But as a great tide of new wounded soldiers flooded into the hospital, they decided to accept her help. Her first request was for two hundred scrub brushes.

Florence and her nurses worked like slaves cleaning the hospital, getting clean bedding and clothing for the soldiers, and serving healthy food. The percentage of men who got well multiplied.

She often spent twenty hours a day doing everything she could to ease the soldiers' pain. After she dismissed the other nurses, she would personally tour the wards to see if there was anything the men needed. When more room was needed, she herself paid for a wing to be added. The soldiers' letters home told of her kindness and how much they loved and appreciated her. Florence became famous.

People back home began sending her money for more supplies. Her family, who had been ashamed of her profession, was caught up in a great wave of pride.

The hospital had been built on top of an old sewer. Florence insisted that it be drained and disinfected. When this was done, the death rate dropped by 80 percent. She separated patients who had contagious disease, and the death rate dropped even lower. But Florence pushed herself too hard. She came down with a fever herself, and her health was never the same.

At the end of the war, she went back to England. She was still not willing to rest, however. Because she had become a national hero, she knew people would now listen when she talked about the need for hospital reforms.

Queen Victoria invited her for a visit and listened to her ideas. Florence suggested that the government set up a commission to study what changes should be made. At that time, women weren't permitted to take such a high office, so her friend Sidney Herbert was put in charge, even though Florence did much of the work.

Next she started a school for nurses in London. She went on to write books on nursing and hospitals. When the Civil War broke out in the United States, she helped organize hospitals for the sick and wounded in the North. She worked until she collapsed and wasn't expected to live. She did live, but she could not walk for six years.

Even that didn't stop her, however. Politicians and hospital administrators came to her for advice, and she continued to write books and reports.

Florence Nightingale lived to be more than ninety. By the time she died, she had won respect for nurses and had revolutionized the way hospitals were run in England—and throughout the world.

DISCUSS

Can you think of a time when you gave up your own comfort or pleasure to serve God or someone else? Can you think of a time when someone did that for you?

60

POCAHONTAS

BLESSED ARE THE PEACEMAKERS, FOR THEY WILL BE
CALLED SONS OF GOD. (MATTHEW 5:9)

While growing up in the late 1500s in what is now Virginia, Pocahontas wondered why her gods didn't answer when she prayed to them. Like the rest of the Algonquin Indians, she worshiped animal spirits, especially the Great Hare. The Algonquins believed the Great Hare had created them. Little did she know that men would one day come in huge boats and teach her about a powerful God who could answer all of her prayers.

At first, Pocahontas was afraid of the white men. She hid behind bushes while she watched them. Then her father, the powerful Chief Powhatan, began trading with their captain, John Smith. Powhatan gave the white men food. They gave him kettles, swords, beads, and hatchets. But the chief was a moody man who became angry when John Smith refused to trade guns.

One day as John was exploring and making maps of the area, a band of Indians captured him. He asked to see Powhatan. But when the chief saw John's maps, he accused him of being a spy and decided to kill him.

Powhatan lunged toward John Smith with his stone war club raised above his head. Before he could strike, however, Pocahontas hurled herself in front of John and begged her father not to kill him.

The chief became angry and told her to move. Even though she had never disobeyed her father and was terrified of what he would do to her, Pocahontas refused until he agreed not to hurt the white man.

Powhatan eventually cooled off and let John go. Later, he even began sending food to the settlers every week, and he allowed Pocahontas to go along. John Smith, the Reverend Hunt, and the boys in the settlement became her friends. The minister told Pocahontas that the true God was like a father. He loved all of His children. He explained how God had sent Jesus to die to save all the tribes of the world.

It wasn't long before Powhatan became angry at the white men again. He thought too many were coming to his land, carrying guns, and treating him rudely. He stopped trading with them and told Pocahontas she could no longer visit the settlement. And now the chief made plans to have John killed.

Pocahontas heard of the plot and slipped through the forest to warn him—even though tribal law said that anyone caught warning an enemy had to be killed. Chief Powhatan's plan didn't work, and he suspected that Pocahontas was responsible, but he couldn't prove it.

When Pocahontas turned fourteen, her father told her she was to marry a warrior who was the son of another chief. The marriage was short; her husband was killed fighting "white skins."

By 1613, seven hundred settlers were in Virginia, and there were continual problems between the settlers and the Indians. The captain of a trading ship decided to take matters into his own hands, and he kidnapped Pocahontas. He hoped to force her father to return some settlers the Indians had captured and guns they had stolen. Powhatan refused.

Pocahontas was taken to an area where there were five English forts. At first she was homesick and was hurt that her father cared more about guns than he did about her. As soon as she realized that the Great Hare would not help her, either, she became eager to learn more about God. It was during this time that she met John Rolfe, a kind Christian man whose wife and daughter had died. John helped Pocahontas learn to speak English better, and he read the Bible to her.

A year passed. Pocahontas became a Christian and was baptized. She and John grew to love each other, and they planned to marry. She sent word to her father, although she thought he would never forgive her for wanting to live among the whites.

But Powhatan surprised her. Now that she was no longer a hostage, he wouldn't lose face if he made a peace offer. He gave his blessing, saying that their marriage showed friendship between the races. Their wedding brought a time of peace, when settlers were not afraid to leave the forts.

Pocahontas and John had a son. Then their family went to England, because people there were anxious to meet the Indian princess. She was invited to many parties and balls. She met important people, including the king and queen. It was a happy time, but she missed the beautiful forests of Virginia.

They were about to return home when Pocahontas caught smallpox. She died at the age of twenty-two. Although her life was short, she has been remembered ever since for all she did to make peace.

DISCUSS

Have you ever tried to make peace between two people? How? Can you think of anyone who is angry or resentful toward someone else? Is there anything you could do to help the person put his/her differences aside? How could you help someone make peace with God?

NOTES

AUTHOR'S NOTE

1. A. W. Tozer, *Let My People Go: The Life of Robert A. Jaffray*, rev. ed. (Camp Hill, Pa.: Christian Publications, 1990), 1.

DAY 1

1. Jean Watson, *Watchmaker's Daughter* (Old Tappan, N.J.: Revell, 1982), 155.

DAY 2

1. Frank and Janet Ferrell, *Trevor's Place: The Story of the Boy Who Brings Hope to the Homeless* (New York: Harper & Row, 1985), 3.

DAY 3

1. Doris Van Stone with Erwin Lutzer, *Dorie: The Girl Nobody Loved* (Chicago: Moody, 1979), 71.

DAY 4

1. Dave Dravecky and Jan Dravecky, *When You Can't Come Back* (Grand Rapids: Zondervan, 1992), 182.

DAY 5

1. David Shibley and Naomi Shibley, *The Smoke of a Thousand Villages* (Nashville: Thomas Nelson, 1989), 83–88; John D. Woodbridge, ed., *More Than Conquerors* (Chicago: Moody, 1992), 63–68.

DAY 7

1. Carolyn E. Phillips, *Michelle* (Ventura, Calif.: Regal, 1980), 29–30.
2. Ibid., 156.

DAY 10

1. John D. Woodbridge, ed., *More Than Conquerors* (Chicago: Moody, 1992), 224.
2. Ibid.

DAY 12

1. Charles Ludwig, preface to *Susanna Wesley: Mother of John and Charles* (Milford, Mich.: Mott Media, 1984).

DAY 13

1. Crossings Book Club advertisement.

DAY 16

1. A. C. Green with J. C. Webster, *Victory* (Orlando, Fla.: Creation House, 1994), 176.
2. Ibid., 138.

DAY 17

1. Tim Hansel, *You Gotta Keep Dancin'* (Elgin, Ill.: David C. Cook, 1985), 32.
2. Ibid., 39.
3. Personal correspondence from Tim Hansel.
4. Ibid.

DAY 23

1. Kay Cole James with Jacqueline Cobb Fuller, *Never Forget!* (Grand Rapids, Mich.: Zondervan, 1992), 165.

DAY 24

1. Dennis Byrd, *Rise and Walk* (New York: Harper Collins, 1993), 228.

DAY 25

1. Daphne Gray with Gregg Lewis, *Yes, You Can, Heather!* (Grand Rapids, Mich.: Zondervan, 1995), 107.

DAY 27

1. Julie Nixon Eisenhower, *Special People* (New York: Simon & Schuster, 1977), 84.
2. William J. Peterson, *Harriet Beecher Stowe Had a Husband,* (Wheaton, Ill.: Tyndale, 1983), 168.

DAY 28

1. A. Wetherell Johnson, *Created for Commitment* (Wheaton, Ill.: Tyndale, 1982), 200.

DAY 31

1. Literature from Habitat for Humanity.

DAY 34

1 Edith Dean, *Great Women of the Christian Faith* (New York: Harper, 1959), 170.
2. Elliott Wright, *Holy Company: Christian Heroes and Heroines* (New York: Macmillan, 1980), 123.

DAY 35

1. John D. Woodbridge, ed., *More Than Conquerors* (Chicago: Moody, 1992), 52.
2. James C. Hefley, *Heroes of the Faith* (Chicago: Moody, 1963), 184.
3. Dr. and Mrs. Howard Taylor, *Hudson Taylor's Spiritual Secret* (Chicago: Moody, 1932).

DAY 37

1. Mark Shaw, "The Great White Father," *Christian History* 16, no. 40: 44.

DAY 45

1. The selection is from *Gold Cord* by Amy Carmichael, © 1991 The Dohnavur Fellowship, published by Christian Literature Crusade, Fort Washington, Pa. Used by permission.

DAY 47

1. Bob St. John, *The Man Inside Landry* (Waco, Tex.: Word, 1979), 29.

DAY 50

1. Doris Van Stone with Erwin Lutzer, *Dorie: The Girl Nobody Loved* (Chicago: Moody, 1979), 30.
2. Doris Van Stone, on a flier advertising her appearance.

DAY 51

1. Colin Greer, "Our Task Is to Do All We Can—Not to Sit and Wait," *Parade*, 20 October, 1996, 4.
2. John D. Woodbridge, ed., *More Than Conquerors* (Chicago: Moody, 1992), 180.
3. Ibid.
4. Ibid., 181.

DAY 54

1. Wendy Murray Zoba, "Bill Bright's Wonderful Plan for the World," *Christianity Today*, 14 July 1997, 17.
2. Ibid., 26.
3. Ibid., 24.

DAY 55

1. Kenneth N. Taylor, *My Life: A Guided Tour* (Wheaton, Ill.: Tyndale, 1991), 210.
2. Ibid., 96.

DAY 58

1. Harold Morris, *Beyond the Barriers* (Pomona, Calif.: Focus on the Family, 1987), 76.

SELECTED BIBLIOGRAPHY

AYLWARD, GLADYS
Burgess, Alan. *The Small Woman*. Anstey, England: F. A. Thorpe, 1973.

BOOTH, WILLIAM
Jackson, Dave, and Neta Jackson. *Kidnapped by River Rats: William and Catherine Booth*. Minneapolis: Bethany House, 1991.
Jay, Ruth Johnson. *Christians with Courage*. Lincoln, Neb.: Good News Broadcasting, 1973.
Woodbridge, John D. ed. *More Than Conquerors*. Chicago: Moody, 1992.

BRIGHT, BILL
Quebedeaux, Richard. *I Found It!* New York: Harper & Row, 1963.
Woodbridge, John D., ed. *More Than Conquerors*. Chicago: Moody, 1992.

BROTHER ANDREW
"Brother Andrew." *God's Smuggler*. Carmel, N.Y.: Guideposts, 1967.

BUNYAN, JOHN
Arnott, Anne. *Valiant for Truth: The Story of John Bunyan*. Grand Rapids, Mich.: Eerdmans, 1985.
Beal, Rebecca S., "Pulling the Flesh from My Bones." *Christian History* 5, no. 3: 14–35.
Christian History Institute. *Children's Heroes from Christian History Video*. Tape 1. Worcester, Pa.: Gateway Films/Vision Video.
Dengler, Sandy. *John Bunyan*. Chicago: Moody, 1986.

CARMICHAEL, AMY
Elliot, Elisabeth. *A Chance to Die: The Life and Legacy of Amy Carmichael*. Old Tappan, N.J.: Revell, 1987.
Davis, Rebecca Henry. *With Daring Faith*. Greenville, S.C.: Bob Jones Univ. Press, 1987.
Dick, Lois Hoadley. *Amy Carmichael: Let The Little Children Come*. Chicago: Moody, 1984.
Stocker, Fern Neal. *Amy Carmichael*. Chicago: Moody, 1987.

CARVER, GEORGE WASHINGTON
Coil, Suzanne M. *George Washington Carver*. New York: Franklin Watts, 1990.
Jenness, Mary. *The Man Who Asked God Questions*. New York: Friendship, 1946.

CASH, JOHNNY
Cash, Johnny. *Man in Black*. Grand Rapids, Mich.: Zondervan, 179.
Pamplin Jr., Robert B., with Gary K. Eisler. *American Heroes*. New York: Mastermedia, 1995.

COLSON, CHARLES
Wiseman, Stella. *Charles Colson*. Minneapolis: Bethany House, 1995.
Woodbridge, John, D., ed. *More Than Conquerors*. Chicago: Moody, 1992.

DOBSON, JAMES
Focus on the Family newsletters, April 1996, August 1996, December 1998.
Zetterson, Rolf. *Dr. Dobson: Turning Hearts Toward Home*. Dallas: Word, 1989.

DRAVECKY, DAVE
Dravecky, Dave. *Dave Dravecky*. Grand Rapids: Zondervan, 1992.

DRISCOLL, JEAN
Brown Jr., H. Jackson and Robyn Spizman. A *Hero in Every Heart*. Nashville: Thomas Nelson, 1996.
Steffen, Bonnie. "Power Racer on a Roll." *Christian Reader* (July/August 1996).

EARECKSON, JONI
Eareckson, Joni. *Joni*. Minneapolis: Worldwide Pub., 1976.
_____. *Choices, Changes*. Grand Rapids: Zondervan, 1986.
Goetz, Dave. "Joni's Confession." *Christian Reader* (May/June 1996).

ELLIOT, JIM
Elliot, Elisabeth. *The Savage My Kinsman*. New York: Harper & Row, 1961.
_____. *Through Gates of Splendor*. Wheaton, Ill: Tyndale, 1981.
Woodbridge, John D., ed. *More Than Conquerors*. Chicago: Moody, 1992.

FRY, ELIZABETH
Bowie, Walter Russell. *Women of Light*. New York: Harper & Row, 1963.

FULLER, MILLARD
Fuller, Millard, with Diane Scott. *No More Shacks!* Waco, Tex.: Word, 1986.

GRAHAM, BILLY
Gibbs, Nancy, and Richard N. Ostling. "God's Billy Pulpit." Time, 15 November, 1993.
Mitchell, Curtis. *Billy Graham: Saint or Sinner*. Old Tappan, N.J.: Revell, 1979.
Pamplin Jr., Robert B., with Gary K. Eisler. *American Heroes*. New York: Mastermedia, 1995.
Westman, Paul. *Billy Graham: Reaching Out to the World*. Minneapolis: Dillon, 1981.
Wilson, Jean. *Crusader for Christ*. Fort Washington, Pa: Christian Literature Crusade, 1973.

GRAHAM, FRANKLIN
Graham, Franklin. *Rebel with a Cause*. Nashville: Thomas Nelson, 1995.

GRAHAM, RUTH BELL
Mitchell, Curtis. *Billy Graham: Saint or Sinner*. Old Tappan, N.J.: Revell, 1979.
Woodbridge, John D., ed. *Ambassadors for Christ*. Chicago: Moody, 1994.

GREEN, A. C.
A. C. Green, "Faith On and Off the Court." *Decision* (March 1994).

JOHNSON, A. WETHERELL
Woodbridge, John D., ed. *More Than Conquerors*. Chicago: Moody, 1992.

LAMB, SAMUEL
Anderson, Ken. *Bold As a Lamb: Pastor Samuel Lamb and the Underground Church of China*. Grand Rapids, Mich.: Zondervan, 1991.

LANDRY, TOM
Landry, Tom, with Gregg Lewis. *Tom Landry*. Grand Rapids, Mich.: Zondervan, 1990.
Woodbridge, John D., ed. *More Than Conquerors*. Chicago: Moody, 1992.

LIDDELL, ERIC
Magnusson, Sally. *The Flying Scotsman*. New York: Quartet Books, 1981.

LINCOLN, ABRAHAM
Meadowcroft, Enid La Monte. *Abraham Lincoln.* New York: Thomas Y. Crowell, 1942.
Woodbridge, John D., ed. *More Than Conquerors*. Chicago: Moody, 1992.

LIVINGSTONE, DAVID
Austin, Alvyn. "Discovering Livingstone" *Christian History* 16, no. 40:10–19.
Fraser, Antonio, ed. *Heroes and Heroines*. New York: A & W Pub., 1980.
Isichei, Elizabeth. "The Man with Three 'Wives'" *Christian History* 16, no. 40: 28–30.
Larson, Dan. *David Livingstone*. Uhrichsville, Ohio: Barbour, 1992.
Northcott, Cecil. *Livingstone in Africa*. New York: Association, 1957.
Olson, Ted. "The Other Livingstone" *Christian History* 16, no. 40: 32–35.
Wellman, Sam. *David Livingstone*. Uhrichsville, Ohio: Barbour, 1995.

LUTHER, MARTIN
Herzel, Catherine. *Heroes of the Church*. Philadelphia: Lutheran Church Press, 1971.
Hefley, James C. *Heroes of the Faith*. Chicago: Moody, 1963.

McCLARY, CLEBE
McClary, Clebe. *Living Proof.* Atlanta: Cross Roads Books, 1978.

McDOWELL, JOSH
Musser, Joe. *Josh: Excitement of the Unexpected*. San Bernardino, Calif.: Here's Life, 1981.
Woodbridge, John D., ed. *Ambassadors for Christ*. Chicago: Moody, 1994.

MEARS, HENRIETTA
Roe, Earl O. *Dream Big: The Henrietta Mears Story*. Ventura, Calif.: Regal, 1990.
Woodbridge, John D., ed. *More Than Conquerors*. Chicago: Moody, 1992.

MOODY, DWIGHT L.
Bailey, Faith Coxe. *D. L. Moody: The Greatest Evangelist of the Nineteenth Century.* Chicago: Moody, 1959, 1987.
Woodbridge, John D., ed. *More Than Conquerors*. Chicago: Moody, 1992.

MULLER, GEORGE
Miller, Basil. *George Muller.* Grand Rapids: Zondervan, 1941.
Woodbridge, John D., ed. *More Than Conquerors*. Chicago: Moody, 1992.

NEWTON, JOHN
Pollock, John. *Amazing Grace*. San Francisco: Harper & Row, 1981.
Scott, Caroline. *Slave Ship Captain*. Fort Washington, Pa.: Christian Literature Crusade, 1975.

PERKINS, JOHN
Whalin, Terry W. *John Perkins.* Grand Rapids: Zondervan, 1996.

POCAHONTAS
Reece, Colleen L. *Pocahontas: Playful One.* Uhrichsville, Ohio: Barbour, 1995.

ROSE, DARLENE DIEBLER
Rose, Darlene Diebler. *Evidence Not Seen.* San Francisco: Harper & Row, 1988.

SAUNE, ROMULO
Lawton, Kim A. "Four Modern Martyrs" *Christian Reader* (July/August 1996).
Whalin, W. Terry, and Chris Woehr. *One Bright Shining Path.* Wheaton, Ill.: Crossway, 1993.

SCHAEFFER, EDITH
Schaeffer, Edith. *The Tapestry: The Life and Times of Francis and Edith Schaeffer.* Waco, Tex.: Word, 1981.
Parkhurst, L. G., Jr. *Francis and Edith Schaeffer.* Minneapolis: Bethany, 1996.
Woodbridge, John D., ed. *Ambassadors for Christ.* Chicago: Moody, 1994.

SLESSOR, MARY
Jay, Ruth Johnson. *Mary Slessor: White Queen of the Cannibals.* Chicago: Moody, 1985.

TAYLOR, KENNETH N.
Steffen, Bonnie. "Ken Taylor: Giving the World Good Things to Read." *The Christian Reader* (September/October 1993).
Woodbridge, John D., ed. *More Than Conquerors.* Chicago: Moody, 1992.

TESTRAKE, JOHN
Testrake, John. *Triumph over Terror on Flight 847.* Old Tappan, N.J.: Revell, 1987.
_____. "Hero Touched Millions" *Christian American* (May/June 1996): 10.
_____. "Flight 847—My Story," *Guideposts* (May 1986, 2–7).

THIEMAN, LEANN
Thieman, LeAnn, and Carol Dey. *This Must Be My Brother.* Wheaton, Ill.: Victor, 1995.

TYNDALE, WILLIAM
DeLeeuw, Cateau. *William Tyndale.* New York: Association Press, 1955.
Herzel, Catherine. *Heroes of the Church.* Philadelphia: Lutheran Church Press, 1971.
Protestant Reformation Video, Gateway Films/Vision Video. Christian History Institute and Video Curriculum, 1995.

WASHINGTON, GEORGE
Camp, Norma Cournow. *George Washington: Man of Prayer and Courage.* Milford, Mich.: Mott Media, 1983.

WESLEY, SUSANNA
Deen, Edith. *Great Women of the Christian Faith.* New York: Harper, 1959.
Stageberg, Grace Swenson. *Women of Faith.* St. Cloud, Minn.: North Star, 1991.

Wright, Elliott. *Holy Company: Christian Heroes and Heroines*. New York: Macmillan, 1980.

WHITESTONE, HEATHER (MCCALLUM)
Adams, Amy Jennings, with Jan L. Senn. "Breaking the Sound Barrier" *Christian Reader* (September/October 1995).

WIELAND, BOB
Wieland, Bob, with Sarah Nichols. *One Step at a Time: The Remarkable True Story of Bob Wieland*. Grand Rapids: Zondervan, 1989.

WILBERFORCE, WILLIAM
Turner, Charles, ed. *Chosen Vessels*. Ann Arbor, Mich.: Vine Books, 1985.
Woodbridge, John D., ed. *More Than Conquerors*. Chicago: Moody, 1992.

Moody Press, a ministry of Moody Bible Institute, is designed for education, evangelization, and edification. If we may assist you in knowing more about Christ and the Christian life, please write us without obligation: Moody Press, c/o MLM, Chicago, IL 60610.

NOTES

NOTES